Latin America

Travel better, enjoy more

ULYSSES

Travel Guides

Research and composition
Claude-Victor Langlois

Publisher
André Duchesne

Series Director
Daniel Desjardins

Translation
Ana Mercedes Luís

Editor
Stéphane G. Marceau

Page Layout/ Computer Graphics
André Duchesne
Isabelle Lalonde

Editing assistance
Gilberto D'Escoubet Fernández
Luís Eduardo Arguedas
Pierre Daveluy

Photography Cover page
Patrick Escudero

DISTRIBUTORS

U.S.A.: Hunter Publishing, 130 Campus Drive, Edison, NJ 08818, ☎800-255-0343, fax: (732) 417-1744 or 0482, comments@hunterpublishing.com, www.hunterpublishing.com

Canada: Ulysses Travel Guides, 4176 St. Denis Street, Montréal, Québec, H2W 2M5, ☎(514) 843-9882, ext.2232, fax: (514) 843-9448, info@ulysses.ca, www.ulyssesguides.com

Great Britain and Ireland: Roundhouse Publishing, Millstone, Limers Lane, Northam, North Devon, EX39 2RG, ☎1 202 66 54 32, fax: 1 202 66 62 19, roundhouse.group@ukgateway.net

Other countries: Ulysses Travel Guides, 4176 St. Denis Street, Montréal, Québec, H2W 2M5, ☎(514) 843-9882, ext.2232, fax: 514-843-9448, info@ulysses.ca, www.ulyssesguides.com

Canadian Cataloguing-in-Publication Data (see p 6)
© July 2004, Ulysses Travel Guides.
All rights reserved. Printed in Canada
ISBN 2-89464-676-3

TABLE OF CONTENTS

National Library of Canada cataloguing in publication

Main entry under title:

Spanish for better travel in Latin America

2nd ed.

(Ulysses phrasebook)
Translation of: L'espagnol pour mieux voyager en Amérique latine.
Includes index.
For English-speaking travellers.
Text in English and Spanish.
ISBN 2-89464-676-3

1. Spanish language - Conversation and phrase books - English. 2 Spanish
language - Provincialisms - Latin America I. Series.

PC4121.E8613 2004   468.3'421   C2003-942077-9

Acknowledgements

We acknowledge the financial support of the Government of Canada
through the Book Publishing Industry Development Program (BPIDP) for
our publishing activities. We would also like to thank the government of
Québec for its SODEC income tax program for book publication.

SPANISH IN LATIN AMERICA –
EL ESPAÑOL EN AMÉRICA

Spanish spoken in North, Central and South America, as well as in the Caribbean, is called "Latin-American Spanish" which is a little different from "Castilian Spanish" spoken in Spain. And just like all languages, Spanish has its own share of regional subtleties and shades of meaning which you can easily learn to grasp by listening carefully to people. As some sounds have no equivalent in English, we have introduced a simple phonetic transcription system to allow you to pronounce them and be able to communicate with people during your holiday. To make things easier, we have deliberately skipped over the international phonetic alphabet established by specialists (too hard for mere mortals) to give you a "natural and intuitive" system using common or easily recognizable symbols. They are often put together in an unusual way, but with a little practice, you will soon get the knack of it.

The main linguistic aspects common to Latin-American Spanish are the following:

The *seseo*: consonants *c*, *z* and *s* are all pronounced *s*.

The *yeísmo*: consonants *y* and *ll* are both pronounced *y*.

r and *l* are sometimes confused and are both pronounced *l*.

Some consonants such as *d* and *s* are not always pronounced when at the end of a syllable:

> [dedo] [deo]
> [desde] [dehde] [dede]
> [pasas] [pasah] [pasa]

Archaisms: words no longer in usage in Spain, such as *lindo* for *hermoso* (nice).

7

Americanisms: words from Indian languages, which can have different meanings depending on the country: *Guagua*: bus (in Cuba), baby (in Central America)

Voseo: the use of the pronoun *vos* (plural you) instead of *tú* (singular) and the corresponding verb forms for the second person singular: *vos (amás, temés, partís)*. The *voseo* is only used in Argentina and Uruguay, and is unknown elsewhere in Latin America.

Sounds

The syllables in **bold** print indicate the tonic accent (stressed syllable).

Consonants

Consonants are pronounced similarly to English except the following:

/b/   Pronounced **b** or sometimes a soft **v**, depending on the region or the person: *bañadera* [bahnyah**deh**rah] or [vahnyah**deh**rah] (bathtub).

/c/   Pronounced **s** before *e* and *i*: *cerro* [sehrroh]. Pronounced **k** before *a*, *o* and *u*: *carro* [**kah**rroh]. The **c** is also hard before consonants, except for the letter *h* (see below).

/ch/   Pronounced as in English: *leche* [**leh**cheh]. Until 1995, it was considered a separate letter and is still often listed separately in dictionaries and telephone directories.

/d/   Pronounced a soft **d** like in door: *dar* [dahr] (give). **D** is usually not pronounced when at the end of a word.

/g/ Follows rules similar to **c**;
Pronounced **h** before *e* and *i*: *gente* [**heh**nteh].
Pronounced as in English before *a*, *o* and *u*: *golf*.
Pronounced **wa** or with a slight **g** sound before *ua*: *agua*
[**ah**gwah] (water).
The g is also hard before consonants.

/h/ Never pronounced: *hora* [**oh**rah].

/j/ Pronounced as a guttural **h:** *naranja* [nah**rahn**-hah].

/ll/ Pronounced **y** as in *yen*: *llamar* [yah**mahr**]. Until 1995, it
was considered a separate letter and is still often listed
separately in dictionaries and telephone directories.

/ñ/ Pronounced like the **ni** in "onion", or the **ny** in "canyon":
mañana [mah**nyah**nah].

/qu/ Pronounced **k**: *aquí* [ah**kee**].

/r/ Slightly rolled, as the Irish pronunciation of **r**. Always heavily
rolled at the beginning of a word

/rr/ Heavily rolled making a difference with **r**: *carro* [**kah**rroh]
(car). Contrasting with *caro* [**kah**roh] expensive.

/s/ **S** is always pronounced **s**: *casa* [**kah**sah].

/t/ Always pronounced **t**: *ruta* [**roo**tah] (route) and not
[**roo**dah].

/v/ Pronounced **b**: *vino* [**bee**noh].

/z/ Always pronounced **s**: *luz* [loos].

Introduction

Vowels

/a/ Always pronounced **ah** as in "part", and never **ay** as in "day": *faro* [**fah**roh] (headlight, lighthouse).

/e/ Always pronounced **eh** as in "elf" and never **ey** as in "grey" or **ee** as in "key": *helado* [eh**lah**doh], except when it precedes two consonants, in which case it is pronounced **eh**: *encontrar* [enkohn**trahr**].

/i/ Always pronounced **ee**: *cine* [**see**neh].

/o/ Always pronounced **oh** as in "cone": *poco* [**poh**koh].

/u/ Always pronounced **oo**: *frutas* [**froo**tahs].

/y/ Usually pronounced **ee**: *y* (ee), but this consonant can also sound like the **y** in "yen": *playa* [**plah**yah].

PHONETIC TRANSCRIPTIONS USED IN THIS BOOK

In this conversation guide, you will find that words and sentences are divided into three columns or three lines in each section.

The **first column** usually features the word in English.

Facing it, in the **second column**, is the Spanish equivalent.

Finally, the **third column** is reserved for the phonetic transcription, which shows you how to pronounce the word. This phonetic transcription has been developed with English-speakers in mind and is meant to be as simple as possible.

Occasionally, you will also find Spanish words in the first column, their English equivalents in the second column and the phonetic transcription in the third. This will make it easier to find the meaning of a Spanish word you might hear or read.

There are also two **indexes** at the end of the guide. The first lists the English words featured in this guide and the second lists the Spanish words. Don't forget to use them!

You will also notice that sentences, in addition to being translated in Spanish, are followed by a phonetic transcription to help you pronounce them correctly. Below, you will find a **phonetics chart**. Don't forget that each letter is pronounced as in English. For example, the letter _p_ in the phonetics chart is pronounced like the English _p_ and represents the letter _p_ in Spanish; the letter _k_ in the phonetics chart is pronounced like the English _k_, but can be used to represent the Spanish _c_, _k_ or _qu_.

	Consonants	
Sound	**Spelling**	**Phonetic Transcription**
b	_bar_	[bar]
f	_fin_	[feen]
g	_gana_	[**gah**nah]
ge	_gente_	[**hehn**teh]
gi	_gitano_	[hee**tah**noh]
h	_hambre_	[**ahm**breh]
j	_mujer_	[moo**hehr**]
k	_k kilo_	[**kee**loh]
	ca casa	[**kah**sah]
	co color	[koh**lohr**]
	cu cuchara	[koo**chah**rah]
	qu que	[keh]
l	_luz_	[loose]
m	_mal_	[mahl]
n	_no_	[noh]
p	_par_	[pahr]

r (slightly rolled)	*cara*	[**kah**rah]
rr (rolled)	*razón* (at the beginning of a word)	[**rrason**]
	dar (at the end of a word)	[dah**rr**]
	perro	[**peh**rroh]
v	*vino*	[**bee**noh]

Vowels

Sound	Spelling	Phonetic Transcription
a	*baba*	[**ah**bah]
e	*vela*	[**veh**lah]
i	*lima*	[**lee**mah]
o	*ozono*	[oh**soh**noh]
u	*computadora*	[cohmpoota-**dohr**rah]

In vowel combinations, each vowel sound is pronounced separately.

Sound	Spelling	Phonetic Transcription
ae	*aéreo*	[ah**eh**rehoh]
ai	*caimán*	[kahee**mahn**]
ay	*bay*	[**ah**-ee]
au	*autobús*	[ah-ootoh**boos**]
ea	*real*	[rreh**ahl**]
ee	*leer*	[leh**ehr**]
ei	*peinar*	[pehee**nahr**]
eo	*creo*	[**kreh**oh]
eu	*feudal*	[fehoo**dahl**]
ia	*día*	[**dee**ah]
ie	*piedra*	[peee**ehd**rah]
io	*mio*	[**mee**oh]
iu	*ciudad*	[seeoo**dah**]

Introduction

oa	*coa*	[**ko**hah]
oe	*oeste*	[oh**ehs**teh]
oi	*boina*	[**bo**heenah]
oy	*hoy*	[**o**hee]
oo	*coordinar*	[kohohrdee**nahr**]
ua	*grúa*	[**groo**ah]
ue	*puede*	[**pweh**deh]
ui	*fui*	[**foo**ee]
uy	*muy*	[**moo**ee]
uo	*duo*	[**doo**oh]

THE TONIC ACCENT

The Spanish **tonic accent** is **lexical**, which means that the word always has the same stress no matter where it is situated within a sentence. In English, the word loses its stress depending on the group of words (**syntactic accent**).

In Spanish every word has a stressed syllable, the **tonic accent** (not always written), a very important feature necessary for making yourself understood. As most words are stressed on the second to last syllable, an accent written over a given syllable indicates it is stressed, regardless to where it is placed. So a change in the tonic accent changes the meaning of a word or the tense of a verb, as in the following examples:

*canta**rá***	(future)
*can**ta**ra*	(subjunctive)
***cá**ntara*	(noun)
*calcu**ló***	(past tense)
*cal**cu**lo*	(present tense)
***cál**culo*	(noun)
*deposi**tó***	(past tense)
*depo**si**to*	(present tense)
*de**pó**sito*	(noun)

All words ending in a vowel with no written accent are stressed on the second to last syllable: a**mi**go, **ca**sa, **bar**co.

Words ending in **n** or **s** with no written accent are also stressed on the second to last syllable: a**mi**gos, **ha**blan.

All other words ending in a consonant (except **n** or **s**) with no written accent are stressed on the last syllable: alcoh**ol**, ment**ol**, a**zul**, na**riz**, cor**rer**, us**ted**, es**toy**, re**loj**

USEFUL ADVICE

◆ Read aloud.

◆ Listen to Latin-American songs and try to understand some of the words.

◆ Associating ideas will help you remember words and the language system. For example, in Spanish, you will notice that an **o** ending usually indicates a masculine word, whereas an **a** ending is almost always feminine: the name "Julio" (Julio Iglesias) is masculine; "Gloria" (Gloria Estefan) is feminine.

◆ Make links between English and Spanish. For example, "last" is _último_ in Spanish, which resembles the word "ultimate" in English.

◆ Try to identify words stemming from the same simple form: _rápido_ and _rapidamente_ ("quick" and "quickly"). This is an easy way to increase your vocabulary.

MASCULINE AND FEMININE

In Spanish, masculine words usually end in **o** and feminine words, in **a**.

For example:

La luna	**The moon**
El castillo	**The castle**

However there are some exceptions.

For example:

El sol (masculine)	**The sun**
El corazón (masculine)	**The heart**
La mujer (feminine)	**The woman**
La calle (feminine)	**The street**

OMISSION OF THE PERSONAL PRONOUN

In Spanish, the personal pronoun is usually omitted. So, to say "I travel a lot.", you usually say *Viajo mucho* and not, *Yo viajo mucho.*

For example:

Voy a la playa.	**I'm going to the beach.**
Andamos juntos.	**We're going together.**

THE NEGATIVE FORM

The negative form is very easy in Spanish. All you have to do is put **no** before the verb:

No voy a la playa.	**I'm not going to the beach.**
No come carne.	**He (she) doesn't eat meat.**
¿No vienes conmigo?	**Aren't you coming with me?**

The personal pronoun can be used in the negative form to emphasize the meaning. You must therefore insert *no* between the personal pronoun and the verb.

For example:

Tú no vas a la discoteca.	**You aren't going to the discotheque. (The others are going, but not you.)**
Yo no quiero verte.	**I do not want to see you.**

THE DEFINITE ARTICLE

Masculine singular:

el libro	**the book**
el árbol	**the tree**

Feminine singular:

la tienda	**the shop**
la flor	**the flower**

The Spanish plural definite article has a masculine and a feminine form concording with the word they designate.

For example:

Feminine plural:

Las flores	**the flowers**
Las bibliotecas	**the libraries**

Masculine plural:

Los árboles	**the trees**
Los libros	**the books**

THE INDEFINITE ARTICLE

In Spanish, the indefinite article agrees both in gender and number with the noun it modifies:

Masculine:

Un amigo	**a friend**
Unos amigos	**friends, some friends**
Un vaso	**a glass**
Unos vasos	**glasses, some glasses**

Feminine:

Una amiga	**a friend**
Unas amigas	**friends, some friends**
Ola	**wave**
Unas olas	**waves, some waves**

THE SUBJECT PRONOUN

In Spanish, the subject pronouns are similar to those in German, French and Italian:

Person	Singular	Plural
1st	yo (I)	nosotros (we)
2nd	tú* (you),	Vosotros** (you),
	usted (you)	ustedes (you)
3rd	él (he)	ellos (they – masc.)
	ella (she)	ellas (they – fem.)

*As in most European languages, Spanish has a familiar form and a polite form for the second person, both singular and plural.

Vosotros is a Castilian Spanish form practically never used in Latin America. *Ustedes* is the third person plural meaning **you (plural) and is used for both the familiar and the polite form.

The polite form is commonly used for entrance formalities, banking, hotels, restaurants, transportation and shopping. If you are speaking to a single person, use *usted* and the verb in the third person singular:

You are a very good guide.
Usted es muy buen guía.

Do you have a vacant room?
¿Tiene usted una habitación libre?

If you are speaking to several people, use *ustedes* and the verb in the third person plural.

The familiar form is generally used in any other situation.

Tú is the second person singular familiar form meaning **you**:

¿Eres tú?   **Is that you?**

Usted is the third person singular polite form meaning **you**.

Es usted   **Is that you?**

¿Cómo están ustedes?   **How are you?**
                          (plural familiar and polite forms)

THE VERB

In Spanish, verbs are divided into three different groups easily identified by the infinitive endings: **–ar**. **–er**. and **–ir**. As in English, the different tenses and forms stem from the infinitive.

Note that due to space restrictions, we have not included personal pronouns in the verbs section. They should be read as such:

	English	*Español*
1st person singular	**I**	*Yo*
2nd person singular	**You**	*Tú*
3rd person singular	**He, She**	*Él, Ella, Usted*
1st person plural	**We**	*Nosotros (as)*
2nd person plural	**You**	*Vosotros (as)*
3rd person plural	**They**	*Ellos, Ellas, Ustedes*

The Imperative

If you can conjugate regular verbs in the present tense indicative, you will have no trouble giving orders. In Spanish, the imperative familiar form is identical to the third person of this tense. For example:

Please bring my luggage up to the room.
Por favor sube mis maletas a la habitación.

Shut the door.
Cierra la puerta.

If you are using the polite form with *usted*, you must change the ending for the regular verb in the infinitive to:

verbs in *ar*: **e**
verbs in *ir* and *er*: **a**

For example:

Por favor, suba usted mis maletas (subir : suba).

Buy me a ticket, please.
Compre un billete para mi, por favor (comprar: compre).

If you have to give orders to several people, you must replace the ending of the regular verb in the infinitive with:

verbs in *ar*: **en**
verbs in *ir* and *er*: **an**

For example:

Por favor, suban mis maletas (subir : suban).

Speak slowly.
Hablen más despacio (hablar : hablen).

The Past Simple

The past simple tense is frequently used in spoken Spanish. Therefore, for any action that has taken place in the past, you must use the past simple. For example:

Yesterday, we went to the museum.
Ayer, fuimos al museo.

Last year, I earned a lot of money.
El año pasado gané mucho dinero.

The past perfect is used when the period of time being referred to is not over. For example:

Today, we went to the museum.
Hoy hemos ido al museo.

This year, I earned a lot of money.
Este año he ganado mucho dinero.

1st Group (Verbs ending in –ar)

Speak - *hablar*

Infinitive – *Infinitivo*

Simple	*Simple*	**Compound**	*Compuesto*
speak	*hablar*	have spoken	*haber hablado*

Participle – *Participio*

Present	*Presente*	**Past**	*Pasado*
speaking	*hablando*	spoken	*hablado*
		having spoken	*habiendo hablado*

Indicative – *Indicativo*

Present	*Presente*	**Present Continuous**	*Gerundio*
speak	*hablo*	am speaking	*estoy hablando*
speak	*hablas*	are speaking	*estás hablando*
speaks	*habla*	is speaking	*está hablando*
speak	*hablamos*	are speaking	*estamos hablando*
speak	*habláis*	are speaking	*estáis hablando*
speak	*hablan*	are speaking	*están hablando*

Past simple	*Pasado simple*	**Future**	*Futuro*
spoke	*hablé*	will speak	*hablaré*
spoke	*hablaste*	will speak	*hablarás*
spoke	*habló*	will speak	*hablará*
spoke	*hablamos*	will speak	*hablaremos*
spoke	*hablasteis*	will speak	*hablaréis*
spoke	*hablaron*	will speak	*hablarán*

Present Perfect	*Pasado compuesto*	**Past Perfect**	*Pluscuam-perfecto*
have spoken	*he hablado*	had spoken	*había hablado*
have spoken	*has hablado*	had spoken	*habías hablado*
has spoken	*ha hablado*	had spoken	*había hablado*
have spoken	*hemos hablado*	had spoken	*habíamos hablado*
have spoken	*habéis hablado*	had spoken	*habíais hablado*
have spoken	*han hablado*	had spoken	*habían hablado*

Imperfect Past*	*Imperfecto*
spoke (used to speak)	*hablaba*
spoke (used to speak)	*hablabas*
spoke (used to speak)	*hablaba*
spoke (used to speak)	*hablábamos*
spoke (used to speak)	*hablabais*
spoke (used to speak)	*hablaban*

Grammar

23

* The imperfect past has no equivalent in English and is used for past actions happening over an indefinite period of time. It is somewhat like the verbal expression "used to", for example:

I used to drink a lot of coffee.
Tomaba mucho café.

2nd Group (Verbs ending in –er)

Eat – *comer*

Infinitive – *Infinitivo*

Simple	*Simple*	**Compound**	*Compuesto*
eat	comer	have eaten	haber comido

Participle – *Participio*

Present	*Presente*	**Past**	*Pasado*
eating	comiendo	eaten	comido
		having eaten	habiendo comido

Indicative – *Indicativo*

Present	*Presente*	**Present Continuous**	*Gerundio*
eat	como	am eating	estoy comiendo
eat	comes	are eating	estás comiendo
eats	come	is eating	está comiendo
eat	comemos	are eating	estamos comiendo
eat	coméis	are eating	estáis comiendo
eat	comen	are eating	están comiendo

Grammar

24

Past simple	*Pasado simple*	**Future**	*Futuro*
ate	*comí*	will eat	*comeré*
ate	*comiste*	will eat	*comerás*
ate	*comió*	will eat	*comerá*
ate	*comimos*	will eat	*comeremos*
ate	*comisteis*	will eat	*comeréis*
ate	*comieron*	will eat	*comerán*

Present Perfect	*Pasado compuesto*	**Past Perfect**	*Pluscuam-perfecto*
have eaten	*he comido*	had eaten	*había comido*
have eaten	*has comido*	had eaten	*habías comido*
has eaten	*ha comido*	had eaten	*había comido*
have eaten	*hemos comido*	had eaten	*habíamos comido*
have eaten	*habéis comido*	had eaten	*habíais comido*
have eaten	*han comido*	had eaten	*habían comido*

Imperfect Past	*Imperfecto*
ate (used to eat)	*comía*
ate (used to eat)	*comías*
ate (used to eat)	*comía*
ate (used to eat)	*comíamos*
ate (used to eat)	*comíais*
ate (used to eat)	*comían*

3rd Group (Verbs ending in –ir)

Live – *vivir*

Infinitive – *Infinitivo*

Simple	*Simple*	**Compound**	*Compuesto*
live	*vivir*	have lived	*haber vivido*

Participle – *Participio*

Present	*Presente*	Past	*Pasado*
living	*viviendo*	lived	*vivido*
		having lived	*habiendo vivido*

Indicative – *Indicativo*

Present	*Presente*	Present Continuous	*Gerundio*
live	*vivo*	am living	*estoy viviendo*
live	*vives*	are living	*estás viviendo*
lives	*vive*	is living	*está viviendo*
live	*vivimos*	are living	*estamos viviendo*
live	*vivís*	are living	*estáis viviendo*
live	*viven*	are living	*están viviendo*

Past simple	*Pasado simple*	Future	*Futuro*
lived	*viví*	will live	*viviré*
lived	*viviste*	will live	*vivirás*
lived	*vivió*	will live	*vivirá*
lived	*vivimos*	will live	*viviremos*
lived	*vivisteis*	will live	*viviréis*
lived	*vivieron*	will live	*vivirán*

Present Perfect	*Pasado compuesto*	Past Perfect	*Pluscuam-perfecto*
have lived	*he vivido*	had lived	*había vivido*
have lived	*has vivido*	had lived	*habías vivido*
has lived	*ha vivido*	had lived	*había vivido*
have lived	*hemos vivido*	had lived	*habíamos vivido*
have lived	*habéis vivido*	had lived	*habíais vivido*
have lived	*han vivido*	had lived	*habían vivido*

Imperfect **Past**	*Imperfecto*
lived (used to live)	*vivía*
lived (used to live)	*vivías*
lived (used to live)	*vivía*
lived (used to live)	*vivíamos*
lived (used to live)	*vivíais*
lived (used to live)	*vivían*

The verb "to be"

In Spanish, the verb "to be" is translated by two different irregular verbs: *ser* and *estar*.

Ser, in general terms, indicates something considered permanent. For example:

a) Occupation

I'm a doctor.	*Soy médica.*	[soy **meh**deekah]

b) Colour

The dress is blue.	*El vestido es azul.*	[ehl behs**tee**doh ehs ahzool]

c) Aspect

The house is big.	*La casa es grande.*	[lah **kah**sah ehs **grahn**deh]

d) Possession

The passport is María's.	*El pasaporte es de María.*	[ehl pahsah**por**teh ehs deh mah**ree**ah]

e) Origin

You are from Chile.	*Eres de Chile.*	[**eh**res deh **chee**leh]

f) Nationality

Lola is Mexican.	*Lola es Mexicana.*	[lowlah ehs meh-hee**kah**nah]

g) Material

The wallet is of leather.

La cartera es de piel.

[lah kahr**teh**rah ehs deh py**ehl**]

Estar, in general terms, indicates something considered temporary, feelings and state of mind, as well as to indicate the place of a person or object.

a) Temporary things

I'm fine.

Estoy bien.

[ehs**toy** byen]

b) Place of persons or objects

Havana is in Cuba.

La Habana está en Cuba.

[lah**bah**nah es**tah** ehn **koo**bah]

To be – *ser*

Infinitive – *Infinitivo*

Simple	*Simple*	**Compound**	*Compuesto*
be	ser	have been	haber sido

Participle – *Participio*

Present	*Presente*	**Past**	*Pasado*
being	siendo	been	sido
		having been	habiendo sido

Indicative – *Indicativo*

Present	*Presente*	Past simple	*Pasado simple*
am	*soy*	was	*fui*
are	*eres*	were	*fuiste*
is	*es*	was	*fue*
are	*somos*	were	*fuimos*
are	*sois*	were	*fuisteis*
are	*son*	were	*fueron*

Imperfect Past	*Imperfecto*	Future	*Futuro*
was (used to be)	*era*	will be	*seré*
were (used to be)	*eras*	will be	*serás*
was (used to be)	*era*	will be	*será*
were (used to be)	*éramos*	will be	*seremos*
were (used to be)	*erais*	will be	*seréis*
were (used to be)	*eran*	will be	*serán*

Present Perfect	*Pasado compuesto*	Past Perfect	*Pluscuam-perfecto*
have been	*he sido*	had been	*había sido*
have been	*has sido*	had been	*habías sido*
has been	*ha sido*	had been	*había sido*
have been	*hemos sido*	had been	*habíamos sido*
have been	*habéis sido*	had been	*habíais sido*
have been	*han sido*	had been	*habían sido*

Grammar

To be – *estar*

Infinitive – *Infinitivo*

Simple	*Simple*	**Compound**	*Compuesto*
be	*estar*	have been	*haber estado*

Participle – *Participio*

Present	*Presente*	**Past**	*Pasado*
being	*estando*	been	*estado*
		having been	*haber estado*

Indicative – *Indicativo*

Present	*Presente*	**Past simple**	*Pasado simple*
am	*estoy*	was	*estuve*
are	*estás*	were	*estuviste*
is	*está*	was	*estuvo*
are	*estamos*	were	*estuvimos*
are	*estáis*	were	*estuvisteis*
are	*están*	were	*estuvieron*

Imperfect Past	*Imperfecto*	**Future**	*Futuro*
was (used to be)	*estaba*	will be	*estaré*
were (used to be)	*estabas*	will be	*estarás*
was (used to be)	*estaba*	will be	*estarán*
were (used to be)	*estábamos*	will be	*estaremos*
were (used to be)	*estabais*	will be	*estaréis*
were (used to be)	*estaban*	will be	*estarán*

Present Perfect	*Pasado compuesto*	Past Perfect	*Pluscuam- perfecto*
have been	*he estado*	had been	*había estado*
have been	*has estado*	had been	*habías estado*
has been	*ha estado*	had been	*había estado*
have been	*hemos estado*	had been	*habíamos estado*
have been	*habéis estado*	had been	*habíais estado*
have been	*han estado*	had been	*habían estado*

The verb "have"

In Spanish, the verb "have" is translated by the irregular verb *tener* and is conjugated as follows.

have – *tener*

Infinitive – *Infinitivo*

Simple	*Simple*	Compound	*Compuesto*
have	*tener*	have had	*haber tenido*

Participle – *Participio*

Present	*Presente*	Past	*Pasado*
having	*teniendo*	had	*tenido*
		having had	*habiendo tenido*

Indicative – *Indicativo*

Present	*Presente*	Past simple	*Pasado simple*
have	*tengo*	had	*tuve*
have	*tienes*	had	*tuviste*
has	*tiene*	had	*tuvo*
have	*tenemos*	had	*tuvimos*
have	*tenéis*	had	*tuvisteis*
have	*tienen*	had	*tuvieron*

Grammar

Imperfect Past	*Imperfecto*	Future	*Futuro*
had (used to have)	*tenía*	will have	*tendré*
had (used to have)	*tenía*	will have	*tendrás*
had (used to have)	*tenías*	will have	*tendrá*
had (used to have)	*teníamos*	will have	*tendremos*
had (used to have)	*teníais*	will have	*tendréis*
had (used to have)	*tenían*	will have	*tendrán*

Present Perfect	*Pasado compuesto*	Past Perfect	*Pluscuam-perfecto*
have had	*he tenido*	had had	*había tenido*
have had	*has tenido*	had had	*habías tenido*
has had	*ha tenido*	had had	*había tenido*
have had	*hemos tenido*	had had	*habíamos tenido*
have had	*habéis tenido*	had had	*habíais tenido*
have had	*han tenido*	had had	*habían tenido*

Other verbs – *Otros verbos*

Infinitive		
go	*ir*	[eer]
come	*venir*	[behneer]
give	*dar*	[dahr]
can	*poder*	[pohdehr]
want	*querer*	[kehrehr]
ask for	*pedir*	[pehdeer]
obtain	*conseguir*	[kohnsehgeer]
find	*encontrar*	[ehnkohntrahr]

Grammar

32

Present Indicative (Ist Person)

I go, I'm going	*voy*	[boy]
I come	*vengo*	[**behng**-goh]
I give	*doy*	[doy]
I can	*puedo*	[**pweh**doh]
I want	*quiero*	[**kyeh**roh]
I ask for	*pido*	[**pee**doh]
I get	*consigo*	[kohn**see**goh]
I find	*encuentro*	[ehnkw**ehn**troh]

Past simple (Ist Person)

I went	*fui*	[**foo**ee]
I came	*vine*	[**bee**neh]
I gave	*di*	[dee]
I could / I was able to	*pude*	[**poo**deh]
I wanted	*quise*	[**kee**seh]
I asked for	*pedí*	[peh**dee**]
I got	*conseguí*	[kohnseh**gee**]
I found	*encontré*	[ehnkohn**treh**]

Imperfect Past (Ist Person)

I went (I used to go)	*iba*	[**ee**bah]
I came (I used to come)	*venía*	[beh**nee**ah]
I gave (I used to give)	*daba*	[**dah**bah]
I could (I used to be able to)	*podía*	[poh**dee**ah]
I asked for (I used to ask for)	*pedía*	[peh**dee**ah]
I got (I used to get)	*conseguía*	[kohnseh**gee**ah]
I found (I used to find)	*encontraba*	[ehnkohn**trah**bah]

Future (1st Person)

I will go	*iré*	[ee**reh**]
I will come	*vendré*	[behn**dreh**]
I will give	*daré*	[dah**reh**]
I will be able to	*podré*	[poh**dreh**]
I will want	*querré*	[keh**rreh**]
I will ask for	*pediré*	[pehdee**reh**]
I wil get	*conseguiré*	[kohnsehgee**reh**]
I will find	*encontraré*	[ehnkohntrah**reh**]

FREQUENTLY USED WORDS AND EXPRESSIONS
PALABRAS Y EXPRESIONES USUALES

Yes	*Sí*	[see]
No	*No*	[noh]
Maybe	*Puede ser*	[**pweh**de sehr]
Excuse me	*Perdone*	[pehr**doh**neh]
Hello (familiar form) Hi	*¡Hola!*	[**oh**lah]
Hello (morning) Good morning	*Buenos días*	[**bweh**nohs **dee**ahs]
Hello (afternoon) Good afternoon	*Buenas tardes*	[**bweh**nahs **tahr**dehs]
Good evening	*Buenas tardes*	[**bweh**nahs **noh**chehs]
Good night	*Buenas noches*	[**bweh**nahs **noh**chehs]
Goodbye	*¡Adios!*	[ah**dyohs**]
	Hasta la vista	[**ah**stah lah **bee**stah]
	Hasta luego	[**ah**stah **lweh**goh]
Thank you	*Gracias*	[**grah**syahs]
Thank you very much	*Muchas gracias*	[**moo**chahs **grah**syahs]
Please	*Por favor*	[pohr fa**bohr** | pohr fah**vohr**]
You're welcome	*De nada, por nada*	[deh **nah**dah | pohr **nah**dah]
How are you?	*¿Cómo está usted?, ¿Qué tal?*	[**koh**moh eh**stah oo**steh** | keh tahl]

35

Fine, and you?	*Muy bien, ¿y usted?*	[mwee by**ehn**] [ee oo**steh**]
Fine, thank you	*Muy bien, gracias*	[mwee by**ehn** | **grah**syahs]
Where is the hotel...?	*¿Dónde se encuentra el hotel...?*	[**dohn**deh seh ehn**kwehn**trahn ehl oh**tehl**]
Is there a...?	*¿Hay...?*	[ah-ee]
Is there a pool?	*¿Hay una piscina?*	[ah-ee **oo**nah pee**see**nah]
Is it far from here?	*¿Está lejos de aquí?*	[eh**stah** leh-hohs deh ah**kee**]
Is it close to here?	*¿Está cerca de aquí?*	[eh**stah sehr**kah deh ah**kee**]
here	*aquí*	[ah**kee**]
there	*ahí*	[ah**ee**]
right	*a la derecha*	[ah lah deh**reh**chah]
left	*a la izquierda*	[ah lah eesky**ehr**dah]
straight ahead	*derecho, derechito*	[deh**reh**choh | dehreh**chee**toh]
with	*con*	[kohn]
without	*sin*	[seen]
a lot	*mucho*	[**moo**choh]
a little	*poco*	[**poh**koh]
often	*a menudo*	[ah meh**noo**doh]
sometimes	*de tiempo en tiempo*	[deh **tyehm**poh ehn **tyehm**poh]

when	*cuando*	[**kwahn**doh]
very	*muy*	[mwee]
also	*también*	[tahm**byehn**]
above (on, over)	*encima (sobre, por encima de)*	[ehn**see**mah (**soh**breh | pohr ehn**see**mah deh]]
below (under, beneath)	*debajo (bajo, por debajo de)*	[deh**bah**-hoh (**bah**-hoh | pohr deh**bah**-hoh deh]]
above	*arriba*	[ah**rree**bah]
below	*abajo*	[ah**bah**-hoh]

Excuse me, I do not understand.
Discúlpeme, no comprendo.
[dees**kool**pehmeh, noh kohm**prehn**doh]

Could you speak more slowly, please?
¿Puede usted hablar más lentamente, por favor?
[**pweh**deh oo**steh** ah**blahr** mahs lehnta**mehn**teh, pohr fah**bohr**]

Could you repeat that, please?
¿Puede usted repetir, por favor?
[**pweh**deh oo**steh** rehpeh**teer** pohr fah**bohr**]

Do you speak English?
¿Habla usted inglés?
[**ah**blah oo**steh** een**glehs**]

I do not speak Spanish.
Yo no hablo español.
[yoh noh **ah**bloh ehspahn**yol**]

Is there someone here who speaks English?
¿Hay alguien aquí que hable inglés?
[**ah**-ee **ahl**gyehn ah**kee** keh **ah**bleh eeng**lehs**]

Is there someone here who speaks French?
¿Hay alguien aquí que hable francés?
[**ah**-ee **ahl**gyehn ah**kee** keh **ah**bleh frahn**sehs**]

Could you write that out for me?
¿Puede usted escribírmelo?
[**pweh**deh oo**steh** ehskree**beer**mehloh]

What does that mean?
¿Qué quiere decir eso?
[keh **kyeh**reh deh**seer eh**soh]

What does the word... mean?
¿Qué quiere decir la palabra...?
[keh **kyeh**reh deh**seer** lah pah**lah**brah...]

I understand.
Comprendo.
[kohm**prehn**doh]

Do you understand?
¿Comprende usted?
[kohm**prehn**deh oo**steh**]

In English, we say...
En inglés se dice...
[ehn een**glehs** seh **dee**seh]

In French, we say...
En francés se dice...
[ehn frahn**sehs** seh **dee**seh]

Could you show me in this book?
¿Puede usted indicármelo en el libro?
[**pweh**deh oo**steh** eendee**kahr**mehloh ehn ehl **lee**broh]

Could I have...?
¿Puedo tener...?
[**pweh**doh teh**nehr**...]

I would like to have...
Desearía tener...
[dehseh-ah**ree**ah teh**nehr**]

I do not know.
Yo no sé.
[yoh noh **seh**]

COLOURS – *LOS COLORES*

white	*blanco/a*	[**blahn**koh/a]
black	*negro/a*	[**neh**groh/ah]
red	*rojo/a*	[rohHo/a]
green	*verde*	[**behr**deh]

Practical Information

| blue | *azul* | [ah**zool**] |
| yellow | *amarillo* | [ahmah**riyo**] |

NUMBERS – *LOS NÚMEROS*

one	*uno, una*	[**oo**no | **oo**na]
two	*dos*	[dohs]
three	*tres*	[trehs]
four	*cuatro*	[**kwah**troh]
five	*cinco*	[**seen**koh]
six	*seis*	[**seh**-ees]
seven	*siete*	[**syeh**teh]
eight	*ocho*	[**oh**choh]
nine	*nueve*	[**nweh**beh]
ten	*diez*	[dy**ehs**]
eleven	*once*	[**ohn**seh]
twelve	*doce*	[**doh**seh]
thirteen	*trece*	[**treh**seh]
fourteen	*catorce*	[kah**tohr**seh]
fifteen	*quince*	[**keen**seh]
sixteen	*dieciséis*	[dyehsee**seh**-ees]
seventeen	*diecisiete*	[dyehsee**syeh**teh]
eighteen	*dieciocho*	[dyehsee**oh**choh]
nineteen	*diecinueve*	[dyehsee**nweh**beh]
twenty	*veinte*	[**beh**-eenteh]
twenty-one	*veintiuno*	[beh-een**tyoo**noh]
twenty-two	*veintidós*	[beh-eentee**dohs**]
thirty	*treinta*	[**treh**-eentah]

thirty-one	*treinta y uno*	[treh-eentah**yoo**noh]
thirty-two	*treinta y dos*	[treh-eentah-ee**dohs**]
forty	*cuarenta*	[kwah**rehn**tah]
forty-one	*cuarenta y uno*	[kwahrehnta-h**yoo**noh]
fifty	*cincuenta*	[seen**kwehn**tah]
sixty	*sesenta*	[seh**sehn**tah]
seventy	*setenta*	[seh**tehn**tah]
eighty	*ochenta*	[oh**chehn**tah]
ninety	*noventa*	[nohbehn**tah]
one hundred	*cien / ciento*	[syehn | syehntoh]
two hundred	*doscientos*	[dohsyehntohs]
two hundred forty-two	*doscientos cuarenta y dos*	[dohsyehntohs kwahrehnta--eedohs]
five hundred	*quinientos*	[keenyehntohs]
one thousand	*mil*	[meel]
ten thousand	*diez mil*	[dyehs meel]
one million	*un millón*	[oon meeyohn]

For "thirty" and "forty," as you can see above, and other numbers up to "ninety," you must to add (y + uno, dos, tres, etc.) to the number. Starting at "one hundred," you don't.

TIME – *HORA Y TIEMPO*

Time – *Hora*

What time is it?	*¿Qué hora es ?*	[keh **oh**rah ehs]
It is one o'clock.	*Es la una.*	[ehs lah **oo**nah]
It is two o'clock.	*Son las dos.*	[sohn lahs dohs]

Practical Information

three thirty / half past three	*tres y media*	[trehsee**meh**dyah]
four fifteen / a quarter after four	*cuatro y cuarto*	[**kwah**troh ee **kwah**troh]
four forty-five / a quarter to five	*cinco menos cuarto*	[**seen**koh **meh**nohs **kwahr**toh]
five after six	*seis y cinco*	[**seh**-ees ee **seen**koh]
ten to seven	*siete menos diez*	[**syeh**teh **meh**nohs dyehs]
In fifteen minutes / in a quarter of an hour	*En un cuarto de hora*	[ehn oon **kwahr**toh deh **oh**rah]
In thirty minutes / in a half an hour	*En media hora*	[ehn **meh**dyah **oh**rah]
In an hour	*En una hora*	[ehn **oo**nah **oh**rah]
In a minute	*En un instante, En un momento*	[ehn oon een**stahn**teh ǀ ehn oon moh**mehn**toh]
One moment please	*Un momento, por favor*	[oon moh**mehn**toh ǀ pohr fa**bohr**]
When?	*¿Cuándo?*	[**kwahn**doh]
Right away	*Enseguida*	[ehnseh**gee**dah]
now	*Ahora*	[ah-**oh**rah]
next	*Después*	[dehspoo**ehs**]
later	*Más tarde*	[mahs **tahr**deh]
I will come back in an hour.	*Volveré en una hora.*	[bohlbeh**reh** ehn **oo**nah **oh**rah]

Time of day – *Momentos del día*

day	*día*	[**dee**ah]
night	*noche*	[**noh**cheh]
morning	*mañana*	[mah**nyah**nah]
afternoon	*tarde*	[**tahr**deh]
evening	*tarde*	[**tahr**deh]
today	*hoy*	[**oh**-ee]
this morning	*esta mañana*	[**eh**stah mah**nyah**nah]
this afternoon	*esta tarde*	[**eh**stah **tahr**deh]
this evening	*esta noche*	[**eh**stah **noh**cheh]
tomorrow	*mañana*	[mah**nyah**nah]
tomorrow morning	*mañana por la mañana*	[mah**nyah**nah pohr lah mah**nyah**nah]
tomorrow afternoon	*mañana por la tarde*	[mah**nyah**nah pohr lah **tahr**deh]
tomorrow night	*mañana por la noche*	[mah**nyah**nah pohr lah **noh**cheh]
the day after tomorrow	*pasado mañana*	[pah**sah**doh mah**nyah**nah]
yesterday	*ayer*	[ah**yehr**]
the day before yesterday	*anteayer*	[ahnteh-ah**yehr**]
week	*semana*	[seh**mah**nah]
next week	*la semana próxima*	[lah seh**mah**nah **prohk**seemah]
last week	*la semana pasada*	[lah seh**mah**nah pah**sah**dah]
next Monday	*el lunes próximo*	[ehl **loo**nehs **prohk**seemoh]

Days of the week – *Días de la semana*

Sunday	*domingo*	[doh**meen**goh]
Monday	*lunes*	[**loo**nehs]
Tuesday	*martes*	[**mahr**tehs]
Wednesday	*miércoles*	[my**ehr**kohlehs]
Thursday	*jueves*	[**hweh**behs]
Friday	*viernes*	[by**ehr**nehs]
Saturday	*sábado*	[**sah**bahdoh]

Months – *Meses*

January	*enero*	[eh**neh**roh]
February	*febrero*	[feh**breh**roh]
March	*marzo*	[**mahr**soh]
April	*abril*	[ah**breel**]
May	*mayo*	[**mah**yoh]
June	*junio*	[**hoo**nyoh]
July	*julio*	[**hoo**lyoh]
August	*agosto*	[ah**gohs**toh]
September	*septiembre*	[sehp**tyehm**breh]
October	*octubre*	[ohk**too**breh]
November	*noviembre*	[nohby**ehm**breh]
December	*diciembre*	[dees**yehm**breh]
June 1st	*el primero de junio*	[ehl pree**meh**roh deh **hoo**nyoh]
June 10	*el diez de junio*	[ehl dyehs deh **hoo**nyoh]
June 17	*el diecisiete de junio*	[ehl dyehsees**yeh**teh deh **hoo**nyoh]

July 31	*el treinta y uno de julio*	[ehl trehyntah**yoo**noh deh **hoo**lyoh]
month	*mes*	[mehs]
next month	*el mes próximo*	[ehl mehs **proh**kseemoh]
last month	*el mes pasado*	[ehl mehs pa**sah**doh]
year	*año*	[**ah**nyoh]
next year	*el próximo año*	[ehl **proh**kseemoh **ah**nyoh]
last year	*el año pasado*	[ehl **ah**nyoh pah**sah**doh]

When can we have breakfast?
¿A partir de qué hora se puede desayunar?
[ah pahr**teer** deh keh **oh**rah seh **pweh**deh dehsahyoo**nahr**]

Until what time?
¿Hasta qué hora?
[**ah**stah keh **oh**rah]

When will the room be ready?
¿A qué hora estará lista la habitación?
[ah keh **oh**rah ehstah**rah** lee**stah** lah ahbeetah**syohn**]

When do we have to leave the room?
¿A qué hora se debe dejar la habitación?
[ah keh **oh**rah seh **deh**beh deh-**ahr** lah ahbeetah**syon**]

What is the time difference between... and... ?
¿Cuál es la diferencia de horario entre... y ...?
[kwahl ehs lah deefeh**rehn**syah deh oh**rah**ryoh **ehn**treh... ee...]

Practical Information

COUNTRIES AND NATIONALITIES – *PAISES Y NACIONALIDADES*

Argentina	*Argentina*	[ahr**hen**teenah]
Belgium	*Bélgica*	[**behl**heekah]
Bolivia	*Bolivia*	[bo**lee**byah]
Brazil	*Brasil*	[brah**seel**]
Canada	*Canadá*	[kahnah**dah**]
Chile	*Chile*	[**chee**leh]
Colombia	*Colombia*	[koh**lohm**byah]
Costa Rica	*Costa Rica*	[**koh**stah **rree**kah]
Ecuador	*Ecuador*	[ehkwah**dohr**]
El Salvador	*El Salvador*	[ehl salbah**dohr**]
France	*Francia*	[**frahn**syah]
Guatemala	*Guatemala*	[gwahteh**mah**lah]
Honduras	*Honduras*	[ohn**doo**rahs]
Italy	*Italia*	[ee**tah**lyah]
Mexico	*México*	[**meh**-heekoh]
Nicaragua	*Nicaragua*	[neekah**rah**gwah]
Panamá	*Panamá*	[pahnah**mah**
Paraguay	*Paraguay*	[pahrah**gwah**ee]
Peru	*Perú*	[peh**roo**]
Spain	*España*	[eh**spah**nyah]
Switzerland	*Suiza*	[**swee**sah]
United States	*Estados Unidos*	[eh**stah**dohs oo**nee**dohs]
Uruguay	*Uruguay*	[ooroo**gwah**ee]
Venezuela	*Venezuela*	[behneh**sweh**lah]

I am...	Soy...	[**soy**]
American	Americano/a, Estadounidense	[ahmehree**kah**noh/ah | ehstahdoh-oonee**dehn**seh]
Argentinean	Argentino/a	[ahrhehn**teen**oh/ah]
Belgian	Belga	[**behl**gah]
Bolivian	Boliviano/a	[bohlee**byah**noh/ah]
Brazilian	Brasilero/a	[brahsee**leh**roh/ah]
Canadian	Canadiense	[kahnah**dyehn**seh]
Chilean	Chileno/a	[chee**leh**noh/ah]
Colombian	Colombiano/a	[kohlohm**byah**noh/ah]
Costa Rican	Costarricense	[kohstahrree**sehn**seh]
Ecuadorian	Ecuatoriano/a	[ehkwahtoh-**ryah**noh/ah]
French	Francés/ Francesa	[frahn**sehs** | frahn**seh**sah]
Guatemalan	Guatemalteco/a	[gwahteh-mahl**teh**koh/ah]
Honduran	Hondureño/a	[ohndoo**reh**nyoh/ah]
Italian	Italiano/a	[eetah**lyah**noh/ah]
Mexican	Mexicano/a	[meh-hee**kah**noh/ah]
Nicaraguan	Nicaragüense	[neekahrah**gwehn**seh]
Panamian	Panameño/a	[pahnah**meh**nyoh/ah]
Paraguayan	Paraguayo/a	[pahrah**gwah**yoh/ah]
Peruvian	Peruano/a	[pehroo**ah**noh/ah]
Salvadorian	Salvadoreño/a	[sahlbah-doh**reh**nyoh/ah]
Spanish	Español/a	[ehspah**nyohl**/ah]
Swiss	Suizo/a	[**swee**soh/ah]

| Uruguayan | *Uruguayo/a* | [ooroo**gwah**yoh/ah] |
| Venezuelan | *Venezolano/a* | [behnehsoh**lah**noh/ah] |

ENTRANCE FORMALITIES –
FORMALIDADES DE ENTRADA

bag	*bolso*	[**bohl**soh]
citizen	*ciudadano*	[syoodah**dah**noh]
consulate	*el consulado*	[ehl kohnsoo**lah**doh]
customs	*aduana*	[ah**dwah**nah]
embassy	*la embajada*	[lah ehmbah**hah**dah]
immigration	*inmigración*	[eenmeegrah**syohn**]
luggage	*equipajes*	[ehkee**pah**-heh]
passport	*pasaporte*	[pahsah**pohr**teh]
tourist card	*tarjeta de turismo*	[tahr-**heh**tah deh too**ree**zmoh]
suitcase	*valija, maleta*	[ba**lee**hah | mah**leh**tah]
visa	*visa*	[**bee**sah]

Your passport, please.
Su pasaporte, por favor.
[soo pahsah**pohr**teh pohr fah**bohr**]

How long will you be staying in the country?
¿Cuánto tiempo estará en el país?
[**kwahn**toh **tyehm**poh ehstah**rah** ehn ehl pah-**ees**]

Three days	*Tres días*	[trehs **dee**ahs]
One week	*Una semana*	[**oo**nah seh**mah**nah]
One month	*Un mes*	[oon mehs]

Do you have a return ticket?
¿Tiene usted un billete de vuelta?
[**tyeh**neh oo**steh** oon bee**yeh**teh deh **bwehl**tah]

What is your address while in the country?
¿Cuál será su dirección en el país?
[kwahl seh**rah** soo deerehk**syohn** ehn ehl pah-**ees**]

Are you travelling with children?
¿Viaja usted con niños?
[**byah**-hah oo**steh** kohn **nee**nyohs]

Here is the mother's (father's) permission.
He aquí el permiso de su madre (de su padre).
[eh ah**kee** ehl pehr**mee**soh deh soo **mah**dreh | deh soo **pah**dreh]

I am in transit.
Sólo estoy de pasada.
[eh**stoy** deh pah**sah**dah]

I am on a business trip.
Estoy en viaje de negocios.
[eh**stoy** ehn **byah**-heh deh neh**goh**syohs]

I am just visiting.
Estoy de vacaciones.
[eh**stoy** deh bahkah**syoh**nehs]

Practical Information

?

Could you open your bag, please?
¿Puede usted abrir su bolso, por favor?
[**pweh**deh oo**steh** ah**breer** soo **bohl**soh pohr fah**bohr**]

I have nothing to declare.
Yo no tengo nada que declarar.
[yoh noh **tehn**goh **nah**dah keh dehklah**rahr**]

THE AIRPORT – *EL AEROPUERTO*

airplane	*avión*	[ah**byohn**]
boat	*barco*	[**bahr**koh]
bus	*autobús,* *camión (Mexique),* *guagua (Cuba)*	[ah-ootoh**boos** | kah**myohn** | **gwah**gwah]
car	*automóvil,* *auto, carro,* *máquina*	[ah-ootoh**mohb**eel | **ah**-ootoh | **kah**rroh | **mah**keenah]
rental car	*automóvil,* *auto, carro,* *máquina* *de alquiler*	[ah-ootoh**mohb**eel | **ah**-ootoh | **kah**rroh | **mah**keenah | deh ahlkee**lehr**]
taxi	*taxi*	[**tahk**see]
tourist information	*informaciones* *turísticas*	[eenfohrmah**syoh**nehs too**ree**steekahs]
tourist office	*oficina* *de turismo*	[ohfee**see**nah deh too**reez**moh]
train	*tren*	[trehn]

I have lost a suitcase.
He perdido una maleta.
[eh pehr**dee**doh **oo**nah mah**leh**tah]

I have lost my luggage.
He perdido mi equipaje.
[eh pehr**dee**doh mee ehkee**pah**-heh]

I arrived on flight number... from...
Llegué en el vuelo no... de...
[yeh**geh** ehn ehl **bweh**loh **noo**mehroh... deh...]

I have not got my luggage yet.
Todavía no he recibido mi equipaje.
[tohdah**bee**ah noh eh rehsee**bee**doh mee ehkee**pah**-heh]

Is there a bus to downtown?
¿Hay un autobús que va al centro de la ciudad?
[**ah**-ee oon ah-ootoh**boos** keh **bah** ahl **sehn**troh deh lah **syoo**dah]

Where do I catch it?
¿Dónde se toma?
[**dohn**deh seh **toh**mah]

What is the price for a ticket?
¿Cuánto vale el billete (el tíquet)?
[**kwahn**toh **bah**leh ehl bee**yeh**teh | ehl **tee**keht]

Does this bus go to...?
¿Ese bus va a ...?
[**eh**seh boos bah ah ...]

How long does it take to get to the airport?
¿Cuánto tiempo se necesita para ir al aeropuerto
[**kwahn**toh **tyehm**poh seh nehseh**see**tah **pah**rah eer ahl ah-ehroh**pwehr**toh]

How long does it take to get to downtown?
¿Cuánto tiempo se necesita para ir al centro de la ciudad?
[**kwahn**toh **tyehm**poh seh nehseh**see**tah **pah**rah eer ahl **sehn**troh deh lah **syoo**dah]

How much does it cost?
¿Cuánto cuesta?
[**kwahn**toh **kweh**stah]

Where do I get a taxi?
¿Dónde se toma el taxi?
[**dohn**deh seh **toh**mah ehl **tahk**see]

How much is the trip to...?
¿Cuánto cuesta el trayecto para ir a?
[**kwahn**toh **kweh**stah ehl trah**yehk**toh **pah**rah eer ah...]

Where can I rent a car?
¿Dónde se puede alquilar un auto?
[**dohn**deh seh **pweh**deh ahlkee**lahr** oon **ah**-ootoh]

Is it possible to reserve a hotel room from the airport?
¿Se puede reservar una habitación de hotel desde el aeropuerto?
[seh **pweh**deh rehsehr**bahr** **oo**nah ahbeetah**syohn** deh oh**tehl** **dehz**deh ehl ah-ehroh**pwehr**toh]

Is there a hotel at the airport?
¿Hay un hotel en el aeropuerto?
[**ah**-ee oon oh**tehl** ehn ehl ah-ehroh**pwehr**toh]

Where can I change money?
¿Dónde se puede cambiar dinero?
[**dohn**deh seh **pweh**deh kahm**byahr** dee**neh**roh]

Where are the... offices?
¿Dónde se encuentran las oficinas de...?
[**dohn**deh seh ehn**kwehn**trahn lahs ohfee**see**nahs deh...]

TRANSPORTATION — *LOS TRANSPORTES*

Public transportation – *El transporte colectivo*

air conditioned	*aire acondicionado*	[**ah**-eereh ahkohn-deesyoh**nah**doh]
bus	*bus, autobús, camión (Mexico), guagua (Cuba)*	[boos | ah-ootoh**boos** | kahm**yohn** | **gwah**gwah]
numbered seat	*asiento numerado*	[ah**syehn**toh noomeh**rah**doh]
platform	*andén, muelle*	[ahn**dehn** | **mweh**yeh]
reserved seat	*asiento reservado*	[ah**syehn**toh rehsehr**bah**doh]
restaurant car	*vagón restaurante*	[bah**gohn**-rehstahoo**rahn**teh]
roundtrip ticket	*ida y vuelta*	[**ee**dah ee **bwehl**tah]
station	*estación (de trenes, de bus)*	[ehstah**syohn** deh **treh**nes | deh boos]
subway	*metro*	[**meh**troh]
terminal	*terminal, estación*	[tehrmee**nahl** | ehstah**syohn**]

ticket	*billete, tíquet*	[bee**yeh**teh | **tee**keht]
tour bus	*autocar*	[ah-ootoh**kahr**]
train	*tren*	[trehn]
video	*video*	[bee**deh**-oh]

Where can I buy tickets?
¿Dónde se puede comprar los billetes (tíquetes)?
[**dohn**deh seh **pweh**deh kohm**prahr** lohs bee**yeh**tehs \| tee**keh**tehs]

How much is it for...?
¿Cuánto cuesta el billete para...?
[**kwahn**toh **kweh**stah ehl bee**yeh**teh **pah**rah...]

What is the schedule for...?
¿Cuál es el horario para...?
[**kwahl** ehs ehl oh**rah**reeoh **pah**rah...]

Is there a fare for children?
¿Hay un precio para niños?
[**ah**-ee oon **preh**syoh **pah**rah **nee**nyohs]

What time does the train leave for...?
¿A qué hora sale el tren para...?
[ah keh **oh**rah **sah**leh ehl trehn **pah**rah...]

What time does the bus arrive from...?
¿A qué hora llega el bus de...?
[ah keh **oh**rah **yeh**gah ehl boos deh...]

Is coffee served on board?
¿Se sirve café abordo?
[seh **seer**beh kah**feh** ah**bor**doh]

Is a snack served on board?
¿Se sirve una comida ligera abordo?
[seh **seer**beh oonah koh**mee**dah lee-**heh**rah ah**bor**doh]

Is a meal included in the price of the ticket?
¿La comida está incluida en el precio del billete?
[lah koh**mee**dah ee**stah** een**klwee**dah ehn ehl **preh**syoh dehl bee**yeh**teh]

Which platform for the... train?
¿De cuál andén sale el tren para...?
[deh keh ahn**dehn sah**leh ehl trehn **pah**rah...]

Where do I put my luggage?
¿Dónde ponemos el equipaje?
[**dohn**deh **pohn**goh ehl ehkee**pah**-heh]

Excuse me, you are in my seat.
¿Discúlpeme, usted ocupa mi asiento.
[dees**kool**pehmeh, oo**steh** oh**koo**pah mee ah**syehn**toh]

Which train station are we at?
¿En qué estación estamos?
[ehn keh ehstah**syohn** eh**stah**mohs]

Does this train stop in...?
¿El tren para en...?
[ehl trehn **pah**rah ehn]

The Subway – *Metro*

What is the closest station?
¿Cuál es la estación más cercana?
[kwahl ehs lah ehstah**syohn** mahs sehr**kah**nah]

How much is a ticket?
¿Cuánto cuesta un billete?
[**kwahn**toh **kweh**stah oon bee**yeh**teh]

Is there a booklet of tickets?
¿Hay talonarios de billetes?
[**ah**-ee tahloh**nah**reeohs deh bee**yeh**tehs]

Are there day passes? Weekly passes?
¿Hay tarjetas por un día? una semana?
[**ah**-ee tahr**heh**tahs pohr oon **dee**ah | **oo**nah seh**mah**nah]

Which direction should I take to get to...?
¿Qué dirección hay que tomar para ir a...?
[keh deerehk**syohn ah**-ee keh toh**mahr pah**rah eer ah...]

Do I have to transfer?
¿Hay que hacer una correspondencia (un cambio de...)?
[**ah**-ee keh ah**sehr oo**nah kohrrehspohn**dehn**syah | oon **kahm**byoh deh]

Do you have a map of the subway?
¿Tiene usted un plano del metro?
[**tyeh**neh oos**teh** oon **plah**noh dehl **meh**troh]

When does the subway close?
¿A qué hora cierra el metro?
[ah keh **oh**rah **syeh**rrah ehl **meh**troh]

Driving – *El automóvil*

here	*aquí*	[ak**hee**]
there	*ahí, allí*	[ah-**ee** | ah**yee**]
go ahead / keep going	*avanzar*	[ahbahn**sahr**]
back up	*retroceder*	[rrehtrohseh**dehr**]
straight ahead	*derecho/derechito*	[deh**reh**choh | dehreh**chee**toh]
left	*a la izquierda*	[ah lah ees**kyehr**dah]
right	*a la derecha*	[ah lah deh**reh**chah]
traffic lights	*señales de tránsito*	[seh**nyah**lehs deh **trahn**seetoh]
red light	*semáforo*	[seh**mah**fohroh]
green light	*luz verde*	[loos **behr**deh]
yellow light	*luz anaranjada*	[loos anaran**ha**da]
at the traffic lights	*a las señales de tránsito*	[ah lahs seh**nyah**lehs deh **trahn**seetoh]
intersection	*esquina*	[eh**skee**nah]
traffic circle	*rotonda*	[rroh**tohn**dah]
one way	*sentido único, una sola dirección*	[seh**nteedoh oo**neekoh | **oo**nah **soh**lah deerehk**syohn**]
wrong way	*sentido prohibido, dirección prohibida*	[seh**ntee**doh proheebeedoh | deerehk**syohn** proheebeedah]
drive three kilometres	*haga tres kilómetros*	[**ah**gah trehs kee**loh**mehtrohs]
the second on the right	*la segunda a la derecha*	[lah seh**goon**dah ah lah deh**reh**chah]

| the first | *la primera* | [lah preemehrah |
| on the left | *a la izquierda* | ah lah eeskyehrdah] |

| toll highway | *autopista de peaje* | [ah-ootohpeestah deh peh-ah-heh] |

| dirt road | *carretera sin asfaltar* | [karrehtehrah seen ahsfahltahr] |

| pedestrian street | *calle peatonal* | [kahyeh peh-ahtohnahl] |

Car Rental – *Alquiler*

I would like to rent a car.
Quisiera alquilar un carro.
[keesyehrah ahlkeelahr oon kahrroh]

Do you have an automatic (transmission)?
¿Tiene uno de transmisión automática?
[tyehneh oonoh deh trahnzmeesyohn ah-ootohmahteekah]

Do you have a manual (transmission)?
¿Tiene uno de embriague manual?
[tyehneh oonoh deh ehmbreeahgeh mahnwahl]

How much is it for one day?
¿Cuánto cuesta por un día?
[kwahntoh kwehstah pohr oon deeah]

How much is it for one week?
¿Cuánto cuesta por una semana?
[kwahntoh kwehstah pohr oonah sehmahnah]

Is mileage unlimited?
¿El kilometraje está incluido?
[ehl keelohmeh**trah**-heh eh**stah** een**klwee**doh]

How much is the insurance?
¿Cuánto cuesta el seguro?
[**kwahn**toh **kweh**stah ehl seh**goo**roh]

Is there a deductible for collisions?
¿Hay una penalidad por accidente, por choque?
[**ah**-ee **oo**nah pehnahleedad pohr ahkseedenteh | pohr **choh**keh]

I have a reservation.
Tengo una reservación.
[**tehn**goh **oo**nah rehsehrbah**syohn**]

I have a confirmed rate from the head office.
Tengo un precio confirmado por la compañia.
[**tehn**goh oon **preh**syoh kohnfeer**mah**doh pohr lah kohmpah**nyee**ah]

Mechanics – *Mecánica*

air conditioning	*climatización*	[kleemahteesah**syohn**]
antenna	*antena*	[ahn**teh**nah]
antifreeze	*anticongelante*	[ahntee-kohnheh**lahn**teh]
brakes	*frenos*	[**freh**nohs]
bumper	*parachoques*	[pahrah-**choh**kehs]
cassette	*casete*	[kah**seh**teh]
clutch	*embriague*	[ehmbree**ah**geh]
diesel	*diesel*	[**dyeh**sehl]

electric windows	cristales eléctricos	[kree**stah**lehhs eh**lehk**treekohs]
fan	ventilador	[behnteelah**dohr**]
front (rear) door	puerta, portezuela de delante (de atrás)	[**pwehr**tah | pohrtehs**weh**lah deh deh**lahn**teh | deh ah**trahs**]
fuses	fusibles	[foo**see**blehs]
gas	gasolina, petróleo	[gahsoh**leen**ah | peh**troh**leh-oh]
gear shift	palanca de velocidad	[pah**lahn**kah deh vehlohsee**dah**]
glove compartment	guantera	[gwahn**teh**rah]
hand brake	freno de mano	[**freh**noh deh **mah**noh]
headlight	faro, luz	[**fah**roh | loos]
heater	calefacción	[kahlehfahk**syohn**]
horn	avisador, bocina	[ahbeesah**dohr** | boh**see**nah]
key	llave	[**yah**beh]
lock	cerradura	[sehrrah**doo**rah]
oil	aceite	[ah**seh**-eeteh]
oil filter	filtro de aceite	[**feel**troh deh ah**seh**-eeteh]
pedal	pedal	[peh**dahl**]
radiator	radiador	[rrahdyah**dohr**]
radio	el radio	[ehl **rrah**dyoh]
rear-view mirror	retrovisor	[rrehtrohbee**sohr**]
seat	asiento	[ah**syehn**toh]
starter	arranque	[ah**rrahn**keh]

steering wheel	*volante, timón*	[boh**lahn**teh | tee**mohn**]
sunroof	*techo abrible*	[**the**-choh ah**bree**bleh]
tire	*neumático, goma, llanta*	[neh-oo**mah**teekoh | **goh**mah | **yahn**tah]
trunk	*maletero, guarda maletas*	[mahleh**teh**roh | **gwahr**dah mah**leh**tahs]
turn signal	*intermitente*	[eentehrmee**tehn**teh]
unleaded gas	*gasolina sin plomo*	[gahsoh**lee**nah seen **ploh**moh]
warning light	*piloto*	[pee**loh**toh]
water	*agua*	[**ah**gwah]
windshield	*parabrisa*	[pahrah**bree**sah]
windshield wiper	*limpiaparabrisas*	[leempyah-pahrah**bree**sahs]

aceite	**oil**	[ah**seh**-eeteh]
agua	**water**	[**ah**gwah]
antena	**antenna**	[ahn**teh**nah]
anticongelante	**antifreeze**	[ahntee-kohnheh**lahn**teh]
arranque	**starter**	[ah**rrahn**keh]
asiento	**seat**	[ah**syehn**toh]
avisador	**horn**	[ahbeesah**dohr**]
bocina	**horn**	[boh**see**nah]
calefacción	**heater**	[kahlehfahk**syohn**]

casete	**cassette**	[kah**seh**teh]
cerradura	**lock**	[sehrrah**doo**rah]
climatización	**air conditioning**	[kleemahteesah**syohn**]
cristales eléctricos	**electric windows**	[kree**stah**lehhs eh**lehk**treekohs]
diesel	**diesel**	[**dyeh**sehl]
embriague	**clutch**	[ehmbree**ah**geh]
faro	**headlight**	[**fah**roh]
filtro de aceite	**oil filter**	[**feel**troh deh ah**seh**-eeteh]
frenos	**brakes**	[**freh**nohs]
freno de mano	**hand brake**	[**freh**noh deh **mah**noh]
fusibles	**fuses**	[foo**see**blehs]
goma	**tire**	[**goh**mah]
guarda maletas	**trunk**	[**gwahr**dah mah**leh**tahs]
gasolina	**gas**	[gahsoh**lee**nah]
gasolina sin plomo	**unleaded gas**	[gahsoh**lee**nah seen **ploh**moh]
guantera	**glove compartment**	[gwahn**teh**rah]
intermitente	**turn signal**	[eentehrmee**tehn**teh]
limpiaparabrisas	**windshield wiper**	[leempyah-pahrah**bree**sahs]
llanta	**tire**	[**yahn**tah]
llave	**key**	[**yah**beh]
luz	**headlight**	[loos]
maletero	**trunk**	[mahleh**teh**roh]

neumático	**tire**	[neh-oo**mah**teekoh]
palanca de velocidad	**gear shift**	[pah**lahn**kah deh vehlohsee**dah**]
parabrisa	**windshield**	[pahrah**bree**sah]
parachoques	**bumper**	[pahrah-**choh**kehs]
pedal	**pedal**	[peh**dahl**]
petróleo	**gas**	[peh**troh**leh-oh]
piloto	**warning light**	[pee**loh**toh]
puerta, portezuela de delante (de atrás)	**front (rear) door**	[**pwehr**tah | pohrteh**sweh**lah deh deh**lahn**teh | deh ah**trahs**]
radiador	**radiator**	[rrahdyah**dohr**]
el radio	**radio**	[ehl **rrah**dyoh]
retrovisor	**rear-view mirror**	[rrehtrohbee**sohr**]
techo abrible	**sunroof**	[**the**-choh ah**bree**bleh]
timón	**steering wheel**	[tee**mohn**]
ventilador	**fan**	[behnteelah**dohr**]
volante	**steering wheel**	[boh**lahn**teh]

Filling up – *Echar gasolina, petróleo*

Fill it up, please.
Llene el tanque (depósito), por favor.
[**yeh**neh ehl **tahn**keh \| deh**poh**seetoh \| pohr fah**bohr**]

Put in 50 pesos' worth.
Eche por 50 pesos.
[**eh**-cheh pohr seen**kwehn**tah **peh**sohs]

Check the tire pressure.
Verificar la presión de los neumáticos.
[behreefee**kahr** lah preh**syohn** deh lohs neh-oo**mah**teekohs]

Do you take credit cards?
¿Acepta usted tarjetas de crédito?
[ah**sehp**tah oo**steh** tahr-**heh**tahs dee **kreh**deetoh]

HEALTH – *LA SALUD*

hospital	*hospital*	[ohspee**tahl**]
pharmacy	*farmacia*	[fahr**mah**syah]
doctor	*médico*	[**meh**deekoh]
dentist	*dentista*	[dehn**tee**stah]
It hurts here... / **My... hurts**	*Tengo un dolor...*	[**tehn**goh oon dohl**lohr**]
abdomen	*en el abdomen*	[ehn ehl ahb**doh**mehn]
back	*de espalda*	[deh eh**spahl**dah]
foot	*en el pie*	[ehn ehl pyeh]
head	*de cabeza*	[deh kah**beh**sah]
stomach	*de barriga*	[deh bah**rree**gah]
teeth	*de diente*	[deh **dyehn**teh]
throat	*de garganta*	[deh gahr**gahn**tah]
I am constipated.	*Estoy constipado.*	[eh**stoy** kohnstee**pah**doh]
I have diarrhea.	*Tengo diarrea.*	[**tehn**goh deeahr**reh**-ah]

I have a fever.	*Tengo fiebre.*	[**tehn**goh **fyeh**breh]
My child has a fever.	*Mi hijo tiene fiebre.*	[mee **ee**-hoh **tyeh**neh **fyeh**breh]
I have the flu.	*Tengo gripe.*	[**tehn**goh **gree**peh]

I would like to refill this prescription.
Quisiera renovar esta prescripción.
[kee**syeh**rah rrehnoh**bahr eh**stah prehskreep**syohn**]

Do you have medication for headache?
¿Tiene medicamentos para el dolor de cabeza?
[**tyeh**neh mehdeekah**mehn**tohs **pah**rah ehl doh**lohr** deh kah**beh**sah]

Do you have medication for the flu?
¿Tiene medicamentos para la gripe?
[**tyeh**neh mehdeekah**mehn**tohs **pah**rah lah **gree**peh]

I would like...	*Desearía...*	[dehseh-ah**ree**a]
...cleaning (soaking) solution for soft (hard) contact lenses.	*...una solución para limpiar (mojar) los lentes de contacto suaves (rígidos)*	[**oo**nah sohloos**yohn pah**rah leem**pyahr** | mo-**hahr** | lohs **lehn**tehs deh kohn**tahk**toh **swah**behs | **rree**-heedohs]
...condoms	*...preservativos*	[prehsehrbah**tee**bohs]
...an eyewash	*...un colirio*	[oon koh**lee**reeoh]
...insect bite cream	*...una pomada para las picaduras de insectos*	[**oo**nah poh**mah**dah **pah**rah lahs peekah**door**ahs deh een**sehk**tohs]
...insect repellent	*...un antiinsectos*	[oon **ahn**tee-een**sehk**tohs]

65

| ...malaria pills | ...un medicamento contra la malaria | [oon mehdeekah-**mehn**toh **kohn**trah lah mah**lah**reeah] |
| ...sunblock | ...una crema para el sol | [oonah **kreh**mah **pah**rah ehl sohl] |

EMERGENCIES – *URGENCIAS*

Fire!	¡Fuego!	[**fweh**goh]
Help!	¡Auxilio!	[ah-oo**see**lyoh]
Stop thief!	¡Al ladrón!	[ahl lah**drohn**]
I was attacked.	Me agredieron.	[meh ahgreh**dyeh**rohn]
I was robbed.	Me robaron.	[meh rroh**bah**rohn]

Could you call the police? An ambulance?
¿Puede usted llamar a la policia? ¿la ambulancia?
[**pweh**deh oo**steh** yah**mahr** ah lah pohlee**see**ah | lamboo**lahn**syah?]

Where is the hospital?
¿Dondé está el hospital?
[**dohn**deh eh**stah** ehl ohspee**tahl**]

Can you take me to the hospital?
¿Puede llevarme al hospital?
[**pweh**deh yeh**bahr**meh ahl ohspee**tahl**]

Our luggage was stolen out of our car.
Se robaron nuestro equipaje del carro.
[seh rroh**bah**rohn **nweh**stroh ehkee**pah**-heh dehl **kah**rroh]

My wallet was stolen.
Me robaron la cartera.
[meh rroh**bah**rohn lah kahr**teh**rah]

They had a weapon.
Tenían un arma.
[teh**nee**ahn oon **ahr**mah]

They had a knife.
Tenían un cuchillo.
[teh**nee**ahn oon koo**chee**yoh]

MONEY – *EL DINERO*

bank	*banco*	[**bahn**koh]
exchange bureau	*oficina de cambio*	[ohfee**see**nah deh **kahm**byoh]

What is the exchange rate for the Canadian dollar?
¿Cuál es el cambio para el dólar canadiense?
[kwahl ehs ehl **kahm**byoh **pah**rah ehl **doh**lahr kahnah**dyehn**seh]

American dollar	*dólar americano*	[**doh**lahr ahmehree**kah**noh]
euro	*euro*	[eh**oo**roh]
Swiss franc	*franco suizo*	[**frahn**koh **swee**soh]

I would like to exchange Canadian dollars (American dollars).
Quisiera cambiar dólares canadienses (americanos).
[kee**syeh**rah kahm**byahr doh**lahrehs kahnah**dyehn**sehs | ahmehree**kah**nohs]

I would like to change some travellers cheques.
Quisiera cambiar cheques de viaje.
[kee**syeh**rah kahm**byahr cheh**kehs deh **byah**-heh]

I would like an advance from my credit card.
Quisiera un avance de fondos de mi tarjeta de crédito.
[kee**syeh**rah oon ah**bahn**seh deh **fohn**dohs deh mee tahr**heh**tah deh **kreh**deetoh]

Where can I find an automatic teller machine? A bank machine?
¿Dónde se puede encontrar un cajero automático? ¿una distribuidora de dinero?
[**dohn**deh seh **pweh**deh ehnkohn**trahr** oon kah-**heh**roh ah-ootoh**mah**teekoh | **oo**nah deestreebwee**doh**rah deh dee**neh**roh]

MAIL AND TELEPHONE – *CORREO Y TELÉFONO*

air mail	*por avión*	[pohr ah**byohn**]
express mail	*correo rápido*	[koh**rreh**-oh **rah**peedoh]
stamps	*sellos, estampillas*	[**seh**-yohs | ehstahm**pee**yahs]
weight	*peso*	[**peh**soh]

Where is the post office?
¿Dónde se encuentra el correo?
[**dohn**deh seh ehn**kwehn**trah ehl koh**rreh**-oh]

How much is it to mail a postcard to Canada?
¿Cuánto cuesta un sello para una tarjeta a Canadá?
[**kwahn**toh **kweh**stah oon **seh**yoh **pah**rah **oo**nah tahr**heh**-tah ah kahnah**dah**]

How much is it to mail a letter to Canada?
¿Cuánto cuesta un sello para una carta a Canadá?
[**kwahn**toh **kweh**stah oon **seh**yoh **pah**rah **oo**nah **kahr**tah ah kahnah**dah**]

Where is the telephone office?
¿Dónde está la oficina de teléfonos?
[**dohn**deh eh**stah** lah ohfeesee**nah** deh teh**leh**fohnohs]

Where is the nearest phone booth?
¿Dónde está la cabina de teléfono más cerca?
[**dohn**deh eh**stah** lah kah**bee**nah deh teh**leh**fohnoh mahs **sehr**kah]

How do I make a local call?
¿Cómo se puede hacer una llamada local?
[**koh**moh seh **pweh**deh ah**sehr oo**nah yah**mah**dah loh**kahl**]

How do I call Canada?
¿Cómo se puede hacer una llamada a Canadá?
[**koh**moh seh **pweh**deh ah**sehr oo**nah yamah**dah** ah kahnah**dah**]

I would like to buy a telephone card.
Quisiera comprar una tarjeta de teléfono.
[kee**syeh**rah kohm**prahr oo**na tahr**heh**-ta deh teh**leh**fohnoh]

I would like some change to make a telephone call.
Desearía tener menudo (cambio) para hacer una llamada.
[dehseh-ah**ree**ah teh**nehr** meh**noo**doh | **kahm**byoh | **pah**rah ah**sehr oo**nah yah**mah**dah]

How are telephone calls billed at the hotel?
¿Cómo son facturadas las llamadas en el hotel?
[**koh**moh sohn fahktoo**rah**dahs lahs yah**mah**dahs ehn ehl oh**tehl**]

Practical Information

I am calling Canada Direct, it's a toll-free call.
Llamo a "Canada Direct", es una llamada sin costo.
[**yah**moh ah "kahnah**dah** dee**rehkt**" | ehs **oo**nah yah**mah**dah seen **koh**stoh]

I would like to send a fax.
Quisiera enviar un fax.
[kee**syeh**rah ehm**byahr** oon fahks]

Have you received a fax for me?
¿Recibió un fax para mí?
[rehsee**byoh** oon fahks **pah**rah mee]

ELECTRICITY – *ELECTRICIDAD*

Where can I plug my razor in?
¿Dónde puedo conectar mi máquina de afeitar?
[**dohn**deh **pweh**doh kohnehk**tahr** mee **mah**keenah deh ahfeh-ee**tahr**]

Is the current 220 volts?
¿La corriente es de 220 voltios?
[lah kohrree-**ehn**teh ehs deh dohs**yehn**tohs **beh**-eenteh **bohl**tyos]

The light does not work.
La lámpara no funciona.
[lah **lahm**pahrah noh foon**syoh**nah]

Where can I find batteries for my alarm clock?
¿Dónde puedo comprar pilas para mi despertador?
[**dohn**deh **pweh**doh kohm**prahr** **pee**lahs **pah**rah mee dehspehrtah**dohr**]

Could I plug my computer in here?
¿Puedo conectar mi ordenador aquí?
[**pweh**doh kohnehk**tahr** mee ohrdehnah**dohr** ah**kee**]

Is there a telephone jack for my computer?
¿Hay una toma telefónica para mi ordenador?
[**ah**-ee **oo**nah **toh**mah tehleh**foh**neekah **pah**rah mee ohrdehnah**dohr**]

WEATHER – *EL TIEMPO*

cloudy	*nublado*	[noo**blah**doh]
rain	*la lluvia*	[lah **yoo**byah]
rainy	*lluvioso*	[yoo**byoh**soh]
snow	*la nieve*	[lah **nyeh**beh]
sun	*el sol*	[ehl sohl]
sunny	*soleado*	[sohleh-**ah**doh]
wind	*el viento*	[ehl **byehn**toh]

It's hot out.	*Hace calor.*	[**ah**seh kah**lohr**]
It's cold out.	*Hace frío.*	[**ah**seh **free**oh]
Is it raining?	*¿Llueve?*	[**yweh**beh]
Will it rain?	*¿Va a llover?*	[bah ah yoh**behr**]
Is rain forecasted?	*¿Hay probabilidad de lluvia?*	[**ah**-ee prohbahbeelee**dah** deh **yoo**byah]

la lluvia	**rain**	[lah **yoo**byah]
lluvioso	**rainy**	[yoo**byoh**soh]
la nieve	**snow**	[lah **nyeh**beh]
nublado	**cloudy**	[noo**blah**doh]
el sol	**sun**	[ehl sohl]

soleado	**sunny**	[sohleh-**ah**doh]
el viento	**wind**	[ehl **byehn**toh]

Hace calor.	**It's hot out.**	[**ah**seh kah**lohr**]
Hace frío.	**It's cold out.**	[**ah**seh **free**oh]
¿Llueve?	**Is it raining?**	[**yweh**beh]
¿Va a llover?	**Will it rain?**	[bah ah yoh**behr**]
¿Hay probabilidad de lluvia?	**Is rain forecasted?**	[**ah**-ee prohbahbeelee**dah** deh **yoo**byah]

What is the weather going to be like today?
¿Qué tiempo hará hoy?
[keh **tyehm**poh ah**rah oh**-ee]

It's beautiful out!
¡Qué buen tiempo hace!
[keh bw**ehn tyehm**poh **ah**seh]

It's awful out!
¡Qué mal tiempo!
[keh mahl **tyehm**poh]

HOLIDAYS AND FESTIVALS – *FIESTAS Y FESTIVALES*

Christmas Day	*el día de Navidad*	[**dee**ah deh nahvee**dah**]
New Year's Day	*Año Nuevo*	[**ah**nyoh **nweh**boh]
Epiphany	*día de Reyes*	[**dee**ah deh **reh**yehs]

Mardi Gras / Shrove Tuesday	*Martes de carnaval*	[**mahr**tehs deh kahrnah**bahl**]
Ash Wednesday	*miércoles de ceniza*	[my**ehr**kohlehs deh seh**nee**sah]
Good Friday	*viernes santo*	[**vyehr**nehs **sahn**toh]
Holy Week	*semana santa*	[seh**mah**nah **sahn**tah]
Easter	*el día de Pascua*	[ehl **dee**ah deh **pah**skwah]
May Day	*el día de los trabajadores*	[ehl **dee**ah deh lohs trahbah-hah**doh**rehs]
Mother's Day	*el día de las Madres*	[ehl **dee**ah deh lahs **mah**drehs]
Father's Day	*el día de los Padres*	[ehl **dee**ah deh lohs **pah**drehs]
National Holiday	*la fiesta nacional*	[lah **fyeh**stah nahsyoh**nahl**]
Labour Day	*la fiesta del Trabajo*	[lah **fyeh**stah dehl trah**bah**-hoh]
Thanksgiving	*la Acción de gracia*	[lahk**syohn** deh **grah**syah]
Race Day	*el Día de la raza*	[ehl **dee**ah deeh lah **rrah**sah]

◆ ◆ ◆

día de Navidad	**Christmas Day**	[**dee**ah deh nahvee**dah**]
Año Nuevo	**New Year's Day**	[**ah**nyoh **nweh**boh]
día de Reyes	**Epiphany**	[**dee**ah deh **reh**yehs]
Martes de carnavales	**Mardi Gras / Shrove Tuesday**	[**mahr**tehs deh kahrnah**bahl**]

miércoles de ceniza	**Ash Wednesday**	[my**ehr**kohlehs deh seh**nee**sah]
el día de Pascua	**Easter**	[ehl **dee**ah deh **pah**skwah]
viernes santo	**Good Friday**	[**vyehr**nehs **sahn**toh]
el día de los trabajadores	**May Day**	[ehl **dee**ah deh lohs trahbah-hah**doh**rehs]
el día de las Madres	**Mother's Day**	[ehl **dee**ah deh lahs **mah**drehs
el día de los Padres	**Father's Day**	[ehl **dee**ah deh lohs **pah**drehs]
la fiesta nacional	**National Holiday**	[lah **fyeh**stah nahsyoh**nahl**]
la fiesta del Trabajo	**Labour Day**	[lah **fyeh**stah dehl trah**bah**-hoh]
la Acción de gracia	**Thanksgiving**	[lahk**syohn** deh **grah**syahs]
el Día de la raza	**Race Day**	[ehl **dee**ah deeh lah **rrah**sah]

EXPLORING –
ATRACCIONES TURÍSTICAS

amusement park	*el parque de atracciones*	[ehl **pahr**keh deh ahtrahk**syoh**nehs]
archaeological site	*el centro arqueológico*	[ehl **sehn**troh ahr-kehoh**loh**heekoh]
beach	*la playa*	[lah **plah**yah]
bridge	*el puente*	[ehl **pwehn**teh]
building	*el edificio*	[ehl ehdee**fee**syoh]
cablecar	*el teleférico*	[ehl tehleh**feh**reekoh]
cathedral	*la catedral*	[lah kahteh**drahl**]
central park	*la plaza central*	[lah **plah**sah sehn**trahl**]
church	*la iglesia*	[lah eeg**leh**syah]
city hall	*el ayuntamiento la alcaldía*	[ahyoontah**myehn**toh | lahlkahl**dee**a]
court house	*el palacio de justicia*	[ehl pah**lah**syoh deh hoos**tee**syah]
downtown	*el centro de la ciudad*	[ehl **sehn**troh deh lah **syoo**dah]
falls	*la caída el salto de agua la catarata*	[lah kah-**ee**dah | ehl **sahl**toh deh **ah**gwah | lah kahtah**rah**tah]
fort	*el fuerte*	[ehl **fwehr**teh]
fortress	*la fortaleza*	[lah fohrtah**leh**sah]
fountain	*la fuente*	[lah **fwehn**teh]
funicular railway	*el funicular*	[ehl fooneekoo**lahr**]

historic centre	el centro antiguo, el centro histórico	[ehl **sehn**troh ahn**tee**gwoh] [ehl **sehn**troh ee**stoh**reekoh]
historic port	el puerto viejo	[ehl **pwehr**toh by**eh**-oh]
house	la casa	[lah **kah**sah]
lagoon	la laguna	[lah lah**goo**nah]
lake	el lago	[ehl **lah**goh]
manor	la villa, la casona	[lah **bee**yah | lah kah**soh**nah]
marina	la marina	[lah mah**ree**nah]
market	el mercado	[ehl mehr**kah**doh]
monastery	el monasterio	[ehl mohnah**steh**ryoh]
monument	el monumento	[ehl mohnoo**mehn**toh]
museum	el museo	[ehl moo**seh**-oh]
park	el parque	[ehl **pahr**keh]
pool	la piscina	[lah pee**see**nah]
port	el puerto	[ehl **pwehr**toh]
promenade	la caminata, el paseo	[lah kahmee**nah**tah | ehl pah**seh**-oh]
pyramid	la pirámide	[lah pee**rah**meedeh]
river	el río	[ehl **ree**oh]
ruins	las ruinas	[lahs **rwee**nahs]
sea	el mar, la mar	[ehl mahr | lah mahr]
stadium	el estadio	[ehl eh**stah**dyoh]
statue	la estatua	[lah eh**stah**twah]
temple	el templo	[ehl **tehm**ploh]
theatre	el teatro	[ehl the-**ah**troh]

theme park	*el parque de atracciones*	[ehl **pahr**keh deh ahtrahk**syoh**nehs]
tunnel	*el túnel*	[ehl **too**nehl]
waterfall	*la cascada*	[lah kah**skah**dah]
zoo	*el zoológico*	[ehl soh**loh**-heekoh]

Spanish	English	Pronunciation
el ayuntamiento, la alcadia	**city hall**	[ahyoontah**myehn**toh | lahlkahl**dee**a]
la caída	**falls**	[lah kah-**ee**dah]
la caminata	**promenade**	[lah kahmee**nah**tah]
la casa	**house**	[lah **kah**sah]
la cascada	**waterfall**	[lah kah**skah**dah]
la casona	**manor**	[lah kah**soh**nah]
la catarata	**falls**	[lah kahtah**rah**tah]
la catedral	**cathedral**	[lah kahteh**drahl**]
el centro antiguo	**historic centre**	[ehl **sehn**troh ahn**tee**gwoh]
el centro arqueológico	**archaeological site**	[ehl **sehn**troh ahr-kehoh**loh**heekoh]
el centro de la ciudad	**downtown**	[ehl **sehn**troh deh lah **syoo**dah]
el centro histórico	**historic centre**	[ehl **sehn**troh ees**toh**reekoh]
el edificio	**building**	[ehl ehdee**fee**syoh]
el estadio	**stadium**	[ehl eh**stah**dyoh]
la estatua	**statue**	[lah eh**stah**twah]
la fortaleza	**fortress**	[lah fohrtah**leh**sah]

Exploring

la fuente	**fountain**	[lah **fwehn**teh]
el fuerte	**fort**	[ehl **fwehr**teh]
el funicular	**funicular railway**	[ehl fooneekoo**lahr**]
la iglesia	**church**	[lah ee**gleh**syah]
el lago	**lake**	[ehl lahgoh]
la laguna	**lagoon**	[lah lahgoonah]
la marina	**marina**	[lah mah**ree**nah]
el mar, la mar	**sea**	[ehl mahr | lah mahr]
el mercado	**market**	[ehl mehr**kah**doh]
el monasterio	**monastery**	[ehl mohnah**steh**ryoh]
el monumento	**monument**	[ehl mohnoo**mehn**toh]
el museo	**museum**	[ehl moo**seh**-oh]
el palacio de justicia	**court house**	[ehl pah**lah**syoh deh hoo**stee**syah]
el parque	**park**	[ehl **pahr**keh]
el parque de atracciones	**amusement park / theme park**	[ehl **pahr**keh deh ahtrahk**syoh**nehs]
la piscina	**pool**	[lah pee**see**nah]
el paseo	**promenade**	[ehl pahseh-oh]
la playa	**beach**	[lah **plah**yah]
la plaza central	**central park**	[lah **plah**sah sehn**trahl**]
el puente	**bridge**	[ehl **pwehn**teh]
el puerto	**port / harbour**	[ehl **pwehr**toh]
el puerto viejo	**historic port**	[ehl **pwehr**toh by**eh**-oh]
la pirámide	**pyramid**	[lah pee**rah**meedeh]
el río	**river**	[ehl **ree**oh]

las ruinas	**ruins**	[lahs **rwee**nahs]
el salto de agua	**waterfall**	[ehl **sahl**toh deh **ah**gwah]
el teatro	**theatre**	[ehl the-**ah**troh]
el teleférico	**cablecar**	[ehl tehleh**feh**reekoh]
el templo	**temple**	[ehl **tehm**ploh]
el túnel	**tunnel**	[ehl **too**nehl]
la villa	**manor**	[lah **beey**ah]
el zoológico	**zoo**	[ehl soh**loh**-heekoh]

At the Museum – *En el museo*

19th century	*siglo diecinueve*	[**see**gloh dyehseen**weh**beh]
20th century	*siglo veinte*	[**see**gloh **beh**-eenteh]
21st century	*siglo veintiuno*	[**see**gloh beh-een**tyoo**noh]
African art	*arte africano*	[**ahr**teh ahfree**kah**noh]
Anthropology	*antropología*	[ahntrohpohloh-**hee**ah]
Antiques	*antigüedades*	[ahnteegweh**dah**dehs]
Archaeology	*arqueología*	[ahrkehohloh-**hee**ah]
Architecture	*arquitectura*	[ahrkeetehk**too**rah]
Art Deco	*art decó*	[**ahr**teh **deh**koh]
Art Nouveau	*arte nuevo*	[**ahr**teh **nweh**boh]
Asian art	*arte asiático*	[**ahr**teh ah**syah**teekoh]
Civil War (U.S.)	*guerra de secesión*	[**geh**rrah deh sehseh**syohn**]

Exploring

Colonial art	*arte colonial*	[**ahr**teh kohloh**nyahl**]
Colonial wars	*guerras coloniales*	[**geh**rrahs kohloh**nyahl**ehs]
Colonization	*colonización*	[kohlohneesah**syohn**]
Contemporary art	*arte contemporáneo*	[**ahr**teh kohn-tehmpoh**rah**nehoh]
Decorative arts	*artes decorativas*	[ahrtehs dehkohrah**tee**bahs]
Impressionism	*impresionismo*	[eempreh-syoh**nee**zmoh]
Modern art	*arte moderno*	[**ahr**teh moh**dehr**noh]
Native American art	*arte amerindio*	[**ahr**teh ahmehr**een**dyoh]
Natural sciences	*ciencias naturales*	[**syehn**syahs nahtoo**rah**lehs]
Northerners	*nordistas*	[nohr**dee**stahs]
Paintings	*pinturas*	[peen**too**rahs]
Permanent collection	*colección permanente*	[kohlehk**syohn** pehrmah**nehn**teh]
Pre-columbian art	*arte precolombino*	[**ahr**teh prehkoh-lohm**bee**noh]
Sculptures	*esculturas*	[ehskool**too**rahs]
Southerners	*sudistas, surdistas*	[soo**dee**stahs | soor**dee**stahs]
Spanish period	*periodo hispánico*	[peh**ree**ohdoh ees**pah**neekoh]
Temporary exhibition	*exposición temporal*	[ehkspohsee**syohn** tehmpoh**rahl**]

Urbanism	*urbanismo*	[oorbah**nee**zmoh]
War of independence	*guerra de independencia*	[**geh**rrah deh een-dehpehn**dehn**syah]

antropología	**anthropology**	[ahntrohpohloh-**hee**ah]
antigüedades	**antiques**	[ahnteegweh**dah**dehs]
arqueología	**archaeology**	[ahrkehohloh-**hee**ah]
arquitectura	**architecture**	[ahrkeetehk**too**rah]
art decó	**art Deco**	[**ahr**teh **deh**koh]
arte africano	**African art**	[**ahr**teh ahfree**kah**noh]
arte amerindio	**Native American art**	[**ahr**teh ahmehr**een**dyoh]
arte asiático	**Asian art**	[**ahr**teh ah**syah**teekoh]
arte colonial	**Colonial art**	[**ahr**teh kohloh**nyahl**]
arte contemporáneo	**contemporary art**	[**ahr**teh kohn-tehmpoh**rah**nehoh]
arte moderno	**modern art**	[**ahr**teh moh**dehr**noh]
Arte nuevo	**Art Nouveau**	[**ahr**teh **nweh**boh]
arte precolombino	**Pre-Columbian art**	[**ahr**teh prehkoh-lohm**bee**noh]
artes decorativas	**decorative arts**	[**ahr**tehs dehkohrah**tee**bahs]
ciencias naturales	**natural sciences**	[**syehn**syahs nahtoo**rah**lehs]

Exploring

colección permanente	**permanent collection**	[kohlehk**syohn** pehrmah**nehn**teh]
colonización	**colonization**	[kohlohneesah**syohn**]
esculturas	**sculptures**	[ehskool**too**rahs]
exposición temporal	**temporary exhibition**	[ehkspohsee**syohn** tehmpoh**rahl**]
guerra de secesión	**Civil War (U.S.)**	[**geh**rrah deh sehseh**syohn**]
guerra de independencia	**War of independence**	[**geh**rrah deh eendehpehn**dehn**syah]
guerras coloniales	**colonial wars**	[**geh**rrahs kohloh**nyah**lehs]
impresionismo	**impressionism**	[eempreh-syoh**nee**zmoh]
nordistas	**Northerners**	[nohr**dee**stahs]
periodo hispánico	**Spanish period**	[peh**ree**ohdoh ees**pah**neekoh]
pinturas	**paintings**	[peen**too**rahs]
siglo diecinueve	**19th century**	[**see**gloh dyehseen**weh**beh]
siglo veinte	**20th century**	[**see**gloh beh-eenteh]
siglo veintiuno	**21st century**	[**see**gloh beh-een**tyoo**noh]
sudistas, surdistas	**Southerners**	[soo**dee**stahs | soor**dee**stahs]
urbanismo	**urbanism**	[oorbah**nee**zmoh]

Where is downtown?
¿Dónde se encuentra el centro de la ciudad?
[**dohn**deh seh en**kwehn**trah ehl **sehn**troh deh lah **syoo**dah]

Where is the historic part of town?
¿Dónde se encuentra la ciudad vieja?
[**dohn**deh seh en**kwehn**trah lah syoo**dah byeh**-hah]

Can I walk there from here?
¿Se puede caminar hasta ahí?
[seh **pweh**deh kahmee**nahr** ahstah-**ee**]

What is the best route to get to...?
¿Cuál es el mejor camino para llegar a...?
[kwahl ehs ehl me**hohr** kahmee**noh pah**rah yeh**gahr** ah...]

What is the best way to get to...?
¿Cuál es la mejor manera para llegar a...?
[kwál es la me**hohr** ma**neh**rah **pah**rah yeh**gahr** ah...]

How long will it take?
¿Cuánto tiempo se necesita para llegar a...?
[**kwahn**toh **tyeh**mpoh seh nehseh**see**tah **pah**rah yeh**gahr** ah...]

Where do I catch the bus for downtown?
¿Dónde se toma el bus para el centro de la ciudad?
[**dohn**de seh **toh**mah ehl boos **pah**rah ehl **sehn**troh deh lah syoo**dah**]

Is there a subway station near here?
¿Hay una estación de metro cerca de aquí?
[**ah-ee oo**nah ehstah**syohn** deh **meh**troh **sehr**kah deh ah**kee**]

Do you have a city map?
¿Tiene usted un plano de la ciudad?
[**tyeh**neh oosteh oon **plah**noh deh lah syoo**dah**]

Exploring

I would like a map with an index.
Quisiera un plano con índice.
[kee**syeh**rah oon **plah**noh kohn **een**deeseh]

What is the admission fee?
¿Cuánto cuesta la entrada?
[**kwahn**toh **kweh**stah lah ehn**trah**dah]

Is there a student rate?
¿Hay un precio para estudiante?
[**ah-ee oon pre**hsyoh pahrah ehstoo**dyahn**teh]

Do children have to pay?
¿Los niños deben pagar?
[lohs **nee**nyos **deh**behn pah**gahr**]

What is the museum schedule?
¿Cúal es el horario del museo?
[kwahl ehs ehl oh**rah**reeoh dehl moo**seh**-oh]

Do you have any reading material on the museum?
¿Tiene usted documentación sobre el museo?
[tyehneh oo**steh** dohkoomehntah**syon soh**breh ehl moo**seh**-oh]

Is it permitted to take photographs?
¿Se permite tomar fotos?
[seh pehr**mee**teh toh**mahr foh**tohs]

Where is the coat check?
¿Dónde se encuentra el vestuario?
[**dohn**deh seh ehn**kwehn**trah ehl beh**stwah**reeoh]

Is there a cafe?
¿Hay un café?
[**ah**-ee **oon** kah**feh**]

Where is the painting by...?
¿Dónde se encuentra el cuadro de...?
[**dohn**deh seh en**kwehn**trah ehl **kwah**droh deh...]

What time does the museum close?
¿A qué hora cierra el museo?
[ah keh **oh**rah **syeh**rrah ehl moo**seh**-oh]

OUTDOOR ACTIVITIES –
ACTIVIDADES AL AIRE LIBRE

Where can I...?
¿Dónde se puede practicar...?
[**dohn**deh seh **pweh**deh prahktee**kahr**]

Activities – *Actividades*

play badminton	*el badminton*	[ehl **bahd**meentohn]
go bicycling	*la bicicleta*	[lah beesee**kleh**tah]
go cross-country skiing	*el esquí de fondo*	[ehl eh**skee** deh **fohn**doh]
go diving	*la zambullida*	[lah sahmboo**yee**dah]
go downhill skiing	*el esquí de montaña*	[ehl eh**skee** deh mohn**tahn**yah]
go fishing	*la pesca*	[lah **peh**skah]
play golf	*el golf*	[ehl gohlf]
go hang-gliding	*el parapente*	[ehl pahrah**pehn**teh]
go hiking	*la marcha*	[lah **mahr**chah]
go horseback riding	*la equitación*	[lah ehkeetah**syohn**]
jet-ski	*la motonáutica*	[lah mohtohn**nah**-ooteekah]
ride a motorcycle	*la moto*	[lah **moh**toh]
go mountain biking	*la bicicleta de montaña*	[lah beesee**kleh**tah deh mohn**tahn**yah]
go parachuting	*el paracaidismo*	[ehl pahrahkahee**dee**smo]
go rock climbing	*la escalada*	[lah ehskah**lah**dah]
go sailing	*la vela*	[lah **beh**lah]

go scuba diving	la sumersión, la zambullida	[lah soomehr**syohn** | lah sahmboo**yee**dah]
go snorkelling	submarinismo	[soomahree**nee**smoh]
go snowmobiling	la motonieve	[lah mohtoh**nyeh**beh]
go sport fishing	la pesca deportiva	[lah **peh**skah dehpohr**tee**bah]
go surfing	la plancha de surf	[lah **plahn**chah deh surf]
go swimming	la natación	[lah nahtah**syohn**]
play tennis	el tenis	[ehl **teh**nees]
play volleyball	el volley-ball	[ehl bohlee**bohl**]
go windsurfing	la plancha de vela, tabla de vela	[lah **plahn**chah deh **beh**lah | **tah**blah deh **beh**lah]

Material – *Indumentaria*

air mattress	la balsa	[lah **bahl**sah]
ball	la pelota / el balón	[lah peh**loh**tah | ehl bah**lohn**]
bicycle	la bicicleta	[lah beesee**kleh**tah]
boat	el barco	[ehl **bahr**koh]
boots	los botines	[los boh**tee**nehs]
cabin	la cabina	[lah kah**bee**nah]
deck chair	la silla larga	[lah **seeyah lahr**gah]
fins	las palmas	[las **pahl**mahs]
fishing rod	la caña de pescar	[lah **kahn**yah deh peh**skahr**]
golf clubs	los palos, bates (de golf)	[los **pah**lohs | **bah**tehs deh gohlf]

mask	*la máscara*	[lah **mah**skahrah]
net	*la red*	[lah rehd]
oxygen tank	*la bomba (de echar aire)*	[lah **bohm**bah (deh eht**shahr ahee**reh)]
parasol	*la sombrilla*	[lah sohm**bree**yah]
racket	*la raqueta*	[lah rrah**keh**tah]
rock	*el arrecife*	[ehl ahrreh**see**feh]
sailboat	*el velero*	[ehl beh**leh**roh]
sand	*la arena*	[lah**reh**nah]
ski poles	*los bates*	[lohs **bah**tehs]
skis	*los esquís*	[lohs eh**skees**]
surf board	*la plancha de agua*	[lah **plahn**chah deh **ah**gwah]
windsurfer	*la plancha de vela*	[lah **plahn**chah deh **beh**lah]

The sea – *La mar (ehl mahr)*

calm sea	*mar calmado*	[mahr kahl**mah**doh]
currents	*las corrientes*	[lahs kohree**yehn**tehs]
dangerous currents	*las corrientes peligrosas*	[lahs kohree**yehn**tehs pehlee**groh**sahs]
high tide	*la marea alta*	[lah mah**reh**-ah **ahl**tah]
lifeguard	*el vigilante*	[ehl beehee**lahn**teh]
low tide	*la marea baja*	[lah mah**reh**-ah **bah**hah]
rough sea	*mar agitado*	[mahr ahhee**tah**doh]

Outdoors

ACCOMMODATIONS – *ALOJAMIENTO*

air conditioning	*aire acondicionado, la climatización*	[**ah**-eereh ahkohn-deesyoh**nah**doh | keemah-teesah**syohn**]
apartment-hotel	*el hotel apartamento (residencial)*	[ehl oh**tehl** ahpahr-tah**mehn**toh | rehseedehn**syahl**]
baby	*bebé*	[beh**beh**]
balcony	*balcón*	[bahl**kohn**]
bar	*bar*	[bahr]
bedspread	*un cubrecama, una sobrecama*	[oon koobreh**kah**mah | **oo**nah sohbrehkahmah]
blanket	*una manta*	[**oo**nah **mahn**tah]
blind	*la cortina, el estor*	[lah kohr**tee**nah | ehl eh**stohr**]
boutiques	*tiendas*	[**tyehn**dahs]
chair	*silla*	[**see**yah]
child	*niño*	[**nee**nyoh]
coffeemaker	*la cafetera*	[kahfeh**teh**rah]
corkscrew	*el tirabuzón, sacacorchos*	[teerahboo**sohn** | sahkah**kohr**chos]
curtains	*las cortinas*	[las kohr**tee**nahs]
cutlery	*los cubiertos*	[los koo**byehr**tohs]
dishes	*los platos, la vajilla*	[los **plah**tohs | lah bah-**hee**yah]
dishwasher	*el lavaplatos*	[ehl lahbah**plah**tohs]
double bed	*cama de dos plazas*	[**kah**mah deh **dohs plah**sahs]

double room	*habitación para dos personas*	[ahbeetah**syohn pah**rah **dohs** pehr**soh**nahs]
fan	*el ventilador*	[ehl behnteelah**dohr**]
fax machine	*telecopiadora*	[tehlekohpyah**doh**rah]
freezer	*el congelador*	[kohngehlah**dohr**]
hair-dryer	*secador de pelo*	[sehkah**dohr** deh **peh**loh]
heating	*la calefacción*	[lah kahlehfak**syohn**]
ice cube	*el hielo*	[ehl **yeh**loh]
iron	*la plancha eléctrica*	[lah **plahn**tshah eh**lehk**treekah]
ironing board	*la tabla de planchar*	[lah **tah**blah deh **plahn**tshahr]
kitchenette	*cocinita*	[kochee**nee**tah]
lamp, light	*la luz*	[lah **loos**]
microwave oven	*el horno microondas*	[ehl **ohr**noh meekrohohn**dahs**]
mini-bar	*minibar*	[meenee**bahr**]
noise	*ruido, bulla*	[**rwee**doh | **boo**yah]
noisy	*ruidoso*	[rwee**dohsoh**]
pillow	*una almohada*	[**oo**nah al**mwah**dah]
pillowcase	*una funda de almohada*	[**oo**nah **foon**dah deh ahl**mwah**dah]
pool	*piscina*	[pee**see**na]
privacy	*intimidad*	[eenteemee**dah**]
purified water	*agua purificada*	[**ah**gwah pooreefee**kah**dah]
quiet	*calmado*	[kahl**mah**doh]
radio	*la radio*	[lah **rah**dyoh]

refrigerator	*el refrigerador*	[rehfreegehrah**dohr**]
restaurant	*restaurante*	[rehstahoo**rahn**teh]
room with bathroom	*habitación con baño*	[ahbeetah**syohn** kohn **bahn**yoh]
room with bathtub	*habitación con bañadera*	[ahbeetah**syohn** kohn bahnyah**deh**rah]
room with shower	*habitación con ducha*	[ahbeetah**syohn** kohn doochah]
safe	*la caja de seguridad*	[lah **kah**-hah deh sehgooree**dah**]
sheet	*la sábana*	[lah **sah**bahnah]
single room	*habitación para una persona*	[ahbeetah**syohn** **pah**rah oonah pehr**soh**nah]
soap	*el jabón*	[ehl hah**bohn**]
sofa-bed	*sofá cama*	[soh**fah kah**mah]
stores	*tiendas*	[tyehn**dahs**]
studio	*estudio*	[eh**stoo**dyoh]
suite	*suite*	[sweet]
table	*mesa*	[**meh**sah]
tablecloth	*el mantel*	[ehl mahn**tehl**]
telephone	*teléfono*	[teh**leh**fohnoh]
television	*televisión*	[tehlehbee**syohn**]
television set	*el televisor*	[ehl tehlehbee**sohr**]
towel	*una toalla*	[oonah **twah**yah]
twin beds	*camas separadas*	[**kah**mahs sehpah**rah**dahs]
view of the sea	*vista la mar*	[**vee**stah lah mahr]
view of the city	*vista a la ciudad*	[**vee**stah ah lah syoo**dah**]

view of the mountain	*vista a la montaña*	[**vee**stah ah lah moh**ntah**nyah]
washing machine	*la lavadora*	[lah lahbah**dohr**rah]
window	*ventana*	[behn**tah**nah]

Is there...	*¿Hay...*	[**ah**-ee]
...a pool?	*...una piscina?*	[oonah pee**see**nah]
...a gym?	*...un gimnasio?*	[oon heem**nah**syoh]
...a tennis court?	*...un terreno de tenis?*	[oon teh**rreh**noh deh **teh**nees]
...a golf course?	*...un terreno de golf?*	[oon teh**rreh**noh deh gohlf]
...a marina?	*...una marina?*	[oonah mah**ree**nah]

Do you have a room free for tonight?
¿Tiene usted una habitación libre para esta noche?
[**tyeh**neh oo**steh** oonah ahbeetah**syohn lee**breh **pah**rah **eh**stah **noh**cheh]

How much is the room?
¿Cuál es el precio de la habitación?
[kwahl ehs ehl **preh**syoh deh lah ahbeetah**syohn**]

Is tax included?
¿El impuesto está incluido en el precio?
[ehl eem**pweh**stoh eh**stah** een**klwee**doh ehn ehl **preh**syoh]

We would like a room with a bathroom.
Queremos una habitación con baño.
[keh**reh**mohs oonah ahbeetah**syohn** kohn **bahn**yoh]

Is breakfast included?
¿El desayuno está incluido?
[ehl dehsah**yoo**noh eh**stah** een**klwee**doh]

Do you have any less expensive rooms?
¿Tiene usted habitaciones menos caras?
[**tyeh**neh oo**steh** ahbeetahs**yoh**nehs **meh**nohs **kah**rahs]

Could we see the room?
¿Podemos ver la habitación
[poh**deh**mohs vehr lah ahbeetah**syohn**]

I will take it.
La tomo.
[lah **toh**moh]

I have a reservation in the name of...
Tengo una reservación a nombre de...
[**tehn**goh **oo**nah rrehsehrbah**syohn** ah **nohm**breh deh...]

I have a confirmed rate of...
Se me ha confirmado la tarifa de...
[seh meh ah kohnfeer**mah**doh lah tah**ree**fah deh...]

Do you take credit cards?
¿Acepta usted tarjeta de crédito?
[ah**sehp**tah oo**steh** tahr-**heh**tahs deh **kreh**deetoh]

Would it be possible to have a quieter room?
¿Es posible tener una habitación más tranquila?
[ehs poh**see**bleh teh**nehr** **oo**nah ahbeetah**syohn** mahs trahn**kee**lah]

Creature Comforts

Where can we park the car?
¿Dónde podemos (estacionar, parquear) el carro?
[dohndeh poh**deh**mohs ehstah**syoh**nahr | par**ke**har ehl **kah**rroh]

Could someone help us take our bags to the room?
¿Alguien puede ayudarnos a subir nuestro equipaje?
[**ahl**gyehn **pweh**deh ahyoo**dahr**nohs ah soo**beer** ehl ehkee**pah**-heh]

What time do we have to be out of the room?
¿A qué hora debemos dejar la habitación?
[ah keh **oh**rah deh**beh**mohs deh-**hahr** la ahbeetah**syohn**]

Is the tap water drinkable?
¿Se puede tomar el agua de (la llave, la pila)?
[seh **pweh**deh toh**mahr** ehl **ah**gwah deh lah **yah**beh | lah **pee**lah]

When is breakfast served?
¿De qué hora a qué hora sirven el desayuno?
[deh keh **oh**rah ah keh **oh**rah **seer**behn ehl dehsah**yoo**noh]

Could we change our room?
¿Podríamos cambiar de habitación?
[poh**dree**ahmohs kahm**byahr** deh ahbeetah**syohn**]

We would like a room with a view of the sea.
Quisiéramos una habitación con vista al mar.
[kee**syeh**rahmohs **oo**nah ahbeetah**syohn** kohn **bee**sta ahl mahr]

Could we have two keys?
¿Podemos tener dos llaves?
[poh**deh**mohs teh**nehr** dohs **yah**behs]

What time does the pool close?
¿De qué hora a qué hora está abierta la piscina?
[**ah**stah keh **oh**rah eh**stah** ahb**yehr**tah lah pee**see**nah]

Where can we get towels for the pool?
¿Dónde podemos tomar (pedir) toallas para la piscina?
[**dohn**deh poh**deh**mohs toh**mahr** | peh**deer** | **twah**yahs **pah**rah lah pee**see**nah]

Is there bar service at the pool?
¿Hay un servicio de bar en la piscina?
[**ah**-ee **oon** sehr**bee**syoh deh bahr ehn lah pee**see**nah]

When is the gym open?
¿Cuáles son los horarios del gimnasio?
[**kwah**lehs sohn lohs oh**rah**ryohs dehl heem**nah**syoh]

Is there a safe in the room?
¿Hay una caja fuerte en la habitación?
[**ah**-ee **oo**na **kah**-hah **fwehr**teh ehn lah ahbeetah**syohn**]

Could you wake me up at...?
¿Puede usted despertarme a...?
[**pweh**deh oo**steh** dehspehr**tahr**meh ah]

The air conditioning does not work.
El aire acondicionado no funciona.
[ehl **ah**-eereh ahkohndeesyoh**nah**doh noh foon**syoh**nah]

The toilet is blocked.
El baño está tupido (atascado).
[ehl **bah**nyoh eh**stah** too**pee**doh | ahtah**skah**doh]

There is no electricity..
No hay luz.
[noh **ah**-ee loos]

May I have the key to the safe?
¿Puedo tener la llave del cofre de seguridad?
[**pweh**doh teh**nehr** lah **yah**beh dehl **koh**freh deh sehgooree**dah**]

The telephone does not work.
El teléfono no funciona.
[ehl teh**leh**fohnoh noh foon**syoh**nah]

Do you have any messages for me?
¿Tiene usted mensajes para mí?
[**tyeh**neh oo**steh** mehn**sah**-hehs **pah**rah mee]

Have you received a fax for me?
¿Recibió usted un fax para mí?
[rehsee**byoh** oo**steh** oon fahks **pah**rah mee]

Could you call us a taxi?
¿Puede usted llamarnos un taxi?
[**pweh**deh oo**steh** yah**mahr**nohs oon **tahk**see]

Could you call us a taxi for tomorrow morning at 6am?
¿Puede usted llamarnos un taxi para mañana a las seis?
[**pweh**deh oo**steh** yah**mahr**nohs oon **tahk**see **pah**rah mah**nyah**nah ah lahs **seh**-ees]

We are leaving now.
Partimos ahora.
[pahr**tee**mohs ah-**oh**rah]

Could you get the bill ready?
¿Puede usted preparar la factura?
[**pweh**deh oo**steh** prehpah**rahr** lah fahk**too**rah]

I think there is a mistake on the bill.
Creo que hay un error en la factura.
[**kreh**-oh keh **ah**-ee **oon** eh**rrohr** ehn lah fahk**too**rah]

Could you have our bags brought down?
¿Puede usted hacer bajar nuestro equipaje?
[**pweh**deh oo**steh** ah**sehr** bah-**hahr** **nweh**stroh ehkee**pah**-heh]

Could you keep our bags until...?
¿Puede usted guardar nuestro equipaje hasta...?
[**pweh**deh oo**steh** gwahr**dahr** **nweh**stroh ehkee**pah**-heh **ah**stah]

Thank you for everything, we have had an excellent stay here
Gracias por todo, hemos pasado una excelente estancia con ustedes.
[**grah**syahs pohr **toh**doh, **eh**mohs pah**sah**doh **oo**nah ehkseh**lehn**teh eh**stahn**syah kohn oo**steh**dehs]

We hope to come back soon.
Esperamos volver pronto.
[ehspeh**rah**mohs boh**lvehr prohn**toh]

RESTAURANT – *RESTAURANTE*

Mexican cuisine
La cocina mexicana
[lah koh**see**nah meh-hee**kah**nah]

Could you recommend ... restaurant?
¿Puede recomendarnos un restaurante...?
[**pweh**deh rehkohmehn**dahr**nohs oon rehstah-oo**rahn**teh]

a Chinese	*chino*	[**chee**noh]
a French	*francés*	[frahn**sehs**]
an Indian	*indio*	[**en**deeoh]
an Italian	*italiano*	[eetah**lyah**noh]
a Japanese	*japonés*	[hahpoh**nehs**]

Choosing a table – *Elegir una mesa*

booth	*banqueta*	[bahn**keh**tah]
chair	*silla*	[**see**yah]
dining room	*comedor*	[kohmeh**dohr**]
downstairs	*abajo*	[ah**bah**-hoh]
kitchen	*cocina*	[koh**see**nah]
near the window	*cerca de la ventana*	[**sehr**kah deh lah behn**tah**nah]
patio	*terraza*	[teh**rrah**sah]
table	*mesa*	[**meh**sah]
upstairs	*arriba*	[ah**rree**bah]

| window | *ventana* | [behn**tah**nah] |
| washrooms | *baño* | [**bah**nyoh] |

Dishes – *Platos*

appetizer	*entrante*	[ehn**trahn**teh]
breakfast	*desayuno*	[dehsah**yoo**noh]
cheese	*queso*	[**keh**soh]
dessert	*postre*	[**poh**streh]
dinner	*cena, comida*	[**seh**nah | koh**mee**dah]
dish	*plato*	[**plah**toh]
lunch	*almuerzo*	[ahl**mwehr**soh]
main dish	*plato principal*	[**plah**toh preensee**pahl**]
rice	*arroz*	[ah**rrohs**]
salad	*ensalada*	[ehnsah**lah**dah]
sandwich	*sandwich, emparedado*	[**sahn**gweech | ehmpahreh**dah**doh]
soup	*sopa*	[**soh**pah]
supper	*cena, comida*	[**seh**nah | koh**mee**dah]
vegetarian dishes	*platos vegetarianos*	[**plah**toh behehtahree**ahn**ohs]
au gratin	*tostado, al horno*	[toh**stah**doh | ahl **ohr**noh]
baked	*al horno*	[ahl **ohr**noh]
breaded	*empanizado*	[ehmpahnee**sah**doh]
grilled	*a la parrilla*	[ah lah pah**rree**yah]

Creature Comforts

101

minced	*cortado muy fino*	[kohr**tah**doh mwee **fee**noh]
over a wood fire	*al carbón*	[ahl kahr**bohn**]
roasted	*asado*	[ah**sah**doh]
sauteed	*a la sartén*	[ah lah sahr**tehn**]

Beverages – *Bebidas*

coffee	*café*	[kah**feh**]
coffee with milk	*café con leche*	[kah**feh** kohn **leh**cheh]
cream	*crema*	[**kreh**mah]
espresso	*expreso*	[ehk**spreh**soh]
flat mineral water	*agua mineral*	[**ah**gwah meeneh**rahl**]
herbal tea	*tisana*	[tee**sah**nah]
juice	*jugo*	[**hoo**goh]
milk	*leche*	[**leh**cheh]
mineral water	*agua mineral*	[**ah**gwah meeneh**rahl**]
orange juice	*jugo de naranja*	[**hoo**goh deh nah**rahn**-hah]
purified water	*agua purificada*	[**ah**gwah pooreefee**kah**dah]
soft drink	*coka*	[**koh**kah]
sparkling mineral water	*agua mineral con soda*	[**ah**gwah meeneh**rahl** kohn **soh**dah]
sugar	*azúcar*	[ah**soo**kahr]
tea	*té*	[teh]

Alcoholic drinks – *Licores*

aperitif	*aperitivo*	[ahpehree**tee**boh]
beer	*cerveza*	[sehr**beh**sah]
bottle	*botella*	[boh**teh**yah]
bubbly / sparkling	*espumoso*	[ehspoo**moh**soh]
coffee chaser	*digestivo*	[dee-heh**stee**boh]
dry wine	*vino seco*	[**bee**noh **seh**ko]
house wine	*vino casero, de la casa*	[**bee**noh kah**seh**-roh deh lah **kah**sah]
half	*una media*	[**oo**nah **meh**dyah]
half-bottle	*media botella*	[**meh**dyah boh**teh**yah]
local wine	*vino del país*	[**bee**noh dehl pah-**ees**]
quarter	*un cuarto*	[oon **kwahr**toh]
red wine	*vino tinto*	[**bee**noh **teen**toh]
sweet	*dulce*	[**dool**seh]
white wine	*vino blanco*	[**bee**noh **blahn**koh]
wine	*vino*	[**bee**noh]
wine list	*carta de vinos*	[**kahr**tah deh **bee**nohs]
with ice	*con hielo*	[kohn **yellow**]
without ice	*sin hielo*	[seen **yellow**]

Creature Comforts

Cutlery – *Cubiertos*

ashtray	*el cenicero*	[ehl sehnee**sehr**oh]
cup	*la taza*	[lah **tah**sah]
fork	*el tenedor*	[ehl tehneh**dohr**]
glass	*el vaso*	[ehl **bah**soh]
knife	*el cuchillo*	[ehl koo**chee**yoh]
menu	*el menú*	[ehl meh**noo**]
napkin	*la servilleta*	[lah sehrbee**yeh**tah]
plate	*el plato*	[ehl **plah**toh]
saucer	*el platillo*	[ehl plah**tee**yoh]
spoon	*la cuchara*	[lah koo**chah**rah]

I would like to make a reservation for two people for 8pm.
Quisiera hacer una reservación para dos personas a las 20 horas.
[kees**yeh**rah ah**sehr** oonah rehsehrbah**syohn** pahrah **kwah**troh pehr**soh**nahs ah lahs **beh**-eenteh **oh**rahs]

Will you have room later on?
¿Tendrá usted una mesa más tarde&?
[tehn**drah** oos**teh** oonah **meh**sah mahs **tahr**deh]

I would like to reserve for tomorrow night.
Quisiera reservar para mañana por la noche.
[kees**yeh**rah rehsehr**bahr** pahrah mah**nyah**nah pohr lah **noh**cheh]

When is the restaurant open?
¿Cuáles son los horarios en que está abierto el restaurante ?
[**kwah**lehs **sohn** los o**rah**ryos ehn keh es**tah** abyehrto ehl rehstahoo**ranh**te]

Creature Comforts

Do you take credit cards?
¿Acepta usted tarjetas de crédito?
[ah**sehp**tah oos**teh** tahr**heh**tahs deh **kreh**deetoh]

I would like to see the menu.
Me gustaría ver el menú.
[meh goostah**ree**ah behr ehl meh**noo**]

I would like a table on the patio.
Quiero una mesa en la terraza.
[**kyeh**roh **oo**nah **meh**sah ehn lah teh**rrah**sah]

Could we just have a drink?
¿Podemos simplemente tomar un trago?
[poh**deh**mohs seempleh**mehn**teh toh**mahr** oon **trah**goh]

Could we just have a coffee?
¿Podemos simplemente tomar un café?
[poh**deh**mohs seempleh**mehn**teh toh**mahr** oon kah**feh**]

I am vegetarian.
Soy vegetariano (a).
[soy behehtahree**ah**noh | ah]

I do not eat pork.
No como puerco (cerdo).
[noh **koh**moh **pwehr**koh | **sehr**doh]

I am allergic to nuts.
Soy alérgico a las nueces (a las cacahuetes).
[soy ah**lehr**heekoh ah lahs **nweh**sehs | kahkahwehtehs]

I am allergic to eggs.
Soy alérgico al huevo.
[soy ah**lehr**heekoh ahl **weh**boh]

Do you serve wine by the glass?
¿Puedo tomar sólo un vaso de vino?
[**pweh**doh toh**mahrr soh**loh oon **bah**soh deh **bee**noh]

We did not get...
No hemos tenido...
[noh **eh**mos teh**nee**doh]

I asked for...
Pedí...
[peh**dee**]

It is cold.
Está frío.
[eh**stah free**oh]

It is too salty.
Está muy salado.
[eh**stah** mwee sah**lah**doh]

It is not fresh.
No está fresco.
[noh eh**stah freh**skoh]

The bill / check please.
La cuenta, por favor.
[lah **kwehn**tah, pohr fah**bohr**]

Is the tip included?
¿El servicio está incluido?
[ehl sehr**bee**syoh ehstah een**klwee**doh]

Thank you, it was an excellent meal.
Gracias, fue una excelente comida.
[**grah**syahs, fweh **oo**nah ehkseh**lehn**teh koh**mee**dah]

Thank you, we have had a very pleasant evening.
Gracias, hemos pasado una agradable velada (noche).
[**grah**syahs, **eh**mohs pah**sah**doh **oo**nah ahgrah**dah**bleh beh**lah**dah | **noh**cheh]

Taste – *El sabor*

bitter	*amargo*	[ah**mahr**goh]
bland	*sin sabor*	[seen sah**bohr**]
hot	*picante* *condimentado*	[pee**kahn**teh | kohndeemehn**tah**doh]
mild	*suave*	[**swah**beh]
peppery	*pimentado*	[peemehn**tah**doh]
salty	*salado*	[sah**lah**doh]
spicy	*picante* *condimentado*	[pee**kahn**teh | kohndeemehn**tah**doh]
sweet	*dulce*	[**dool**seh]

◆   ◆   ◆

amargo	**bitter**	[ah**mahr**goh]
condimentado	**hot / spicy**	[kohndeemehn**tah**doh]
dulce	**sweet**	[**dool**seh]
picante	**hot / spicy**	[pee**kahn**teh]

Creature Comforts

pimentado	**peppery**	[peemehn**tah**doh]
salado	**salty**	[sah**lah**doh]
sin sabor	**bland**	[seen sah**bohr**]
suave	**mild**	[**swah**beh]

Spices, Herbs and Condiments – *Especies, yerbas y condimentos*

basil	*hierba buena*	[**yehr**bah **bweh**nah]
(black) pepper	*pimienta*	[pee**myehn**tah]
butter	*mantequilla*	[mahnteh**kee**yah]
cinnamon	*canela*	[kah**neh**lah]
coriander	*culantro, cilantro*	[koo**lahn**troh | see**lahn**troh]
curry	*curry*	[**koo**rree]
ginger	*jengibre*	[hehn**hee**breh]
hot mustard	*mostaza fuerte, picante*	[moh**stah**sah **fwehr**teh | pee**kahn**teh]
hot sauce	*salsa picante*	[**sahl**sah peekahnteh]
mint	*menta*	[**mehn**tah]
nutmeg	*nuez moscada*	[nwehs moh**skah**dah]
pink pepper	*pimienta roja*	[pee**myehn**tah **roh**hah]
rosemary	*romerillo*	[rrohmeh**ree**yoh]
sage	*salvia*	[**sahl**byah]
salt	*sal*	[sahl]
sauce	*salsa*	[**sahl**sah]
sorrel	*acedera*	[ahseh**deh**rah]

soya sauce	*salsa de soja, china*	[**sah**lsah deh **soh**yah | **chee**nah]
spices	*condimento, especie*	[kohndee**mehn**toh | eh**speh**syeh]
spicy	*picante, condimentado/a*	[pee**kahn**teh | kohn-deemehn**tah**doh/ah]
sweet / mild mustard	*mostaza suave*	[moh**stah**sah **swah**beh]
thyme	*tomillo*	[toh**mee**yoh]
vinegar	*vinagre*	[vee**nah**greh]

◆ ◆ ◆

acedera	**sorrel**	[ahseh**deh**rah]
canela	**cinnamon**	[kah**neh**lah]
culantro, cilantro	**coriander**	[koo**lahn**troh | see**lahn**troh]
curry	**curry**	[**koo**rree]
hierba buena	**basil**	[**yehr**bah **bweh**nah]
jengibre	**ginger**	[hehn**hee**breh]
menta	**mint**	[**mehn**tah]
mostaza suave	**sweet / mild mustard**	[moh**stah**sah **swah**beh]
mostaza fuerte, picante	**hot mustard**	[moh**stah**sah **fwehr**teh | pee**kahn**teh]
nuez moscada	**nutmeg**	[nwehs moh**skah**dah]
pimienta	**(black) pepper**	[peem**yehn**tah]
pimienta roja	**pink pepper**	[peem**yehn**tah **roh**hah]
romerillo	**rosemary**	[rrohmeh**ree**yoh]

Creature Comforts

salsa picante	**hot sauce**	[**sahl**sah peekahnteh]
salsa de soja, china	**soya sauce**	[**sahl**sah deh **soh**yah	**chee**nah]
salvia	**sage**	[**sahl**byah]
tomillo	**thyme**	[toh**mee**yoh]
vinagre	**vinegar**	[vee**nah**greh]

Breakfast – *Desayuno*

bread	pan	[pahn]
cheese	queso	[**keh**soh]
coffee	café	[kah**feh**]
croissant	cangrejo, media luna	[kahn**greh**-hoh	**meh**dyah **loo**nah]
eggs	huevos	[**weh**bohs]
French toast	torreja, pan francés	[toh**rreh**-hah	pahn frahn**sehs**]
fruits	frutas	[**froo**tahs]
granola	granola	[grah**noh**lah]
jam	confitura, dulce	[kohnfee**too**rah	**dool**seh]
juice	jugo, zumo	[**hoo**goh	**soo**moh]
marmalade	mermelada	[mehrmeh**lah**dah]
omelette	tortilla	[tohr**tee**yah]
pancakes / crepes	arepas, tortillas, pancake	[ah**reh**pahs	tohr**tee**yahs	pahn**keh**-eek]
pastry	pan de leche, de azúcar	[pahn deh **leh**cheh	deh ah**soo**kahr]

soft cheese	queso fresco	[**keh**soh **freh**skoh]
toasts	tostadas	[toh**stah**dahs]
waffles	gofres	[**goh**frehs]
whole-wheat bread	pan de trigo, pan negro	[pahn deh **tree**goh | pahn **neh**groh]
yogurt	yogur	[yoh**goor**]

◆ ◆ ◆

arepas	**pancakes / crepes**	[ah**reh**pahs]
café	**coffee**	[kah**feh**]
cangrejo	**croissant**	[kahn**greh**-hoh]
confitura	**jam**	[kohnfee**too**rah]
frutas	**fruits**	[**froo**tahs]
gofres	**waffles**	[**goh**frehs]
granola	**granola**	[grah**noh**lah]
huevos	**eggs**	[**weh**bohs]
jugo	**juice**	[**hoo**goh]
media luna	**croissant**	[**mé**dia lo**ú**na]
mermelada	**marmalade**	[mehrmeh**lah**dah]
pan (de leche, de azúcar)	**pastry**	[pahn deh **leh**cheh | deh ah**soo**kahr]
pan	**bread**	[pahn]
pan de trigo, pan negro	**whole-wheat bread**	[pahn deh **tree**goh | pahn **neh**groh]
pan francés	**French toast**	[pahn frahn**sehs**]
queso	**cheese**	[**keh**soh]
queso fresco	**soft cheese**	[**keh**soh **freh**skoh]
torreja	**French toast**	[toh**rreh**-hah]

Creature Comforts

tortilla	**omelette**	[tohr**tee**yah]
tostadas	**toasts**	[tohs**tah**dahs]
yogur	**yogurt**	[yoh**goor**]
zumo	**juice**	[**soo**moh]

Fruits – *Frutas*

apple	*manzana*	[mahn**sah**nah]
apricot	*albaricoque*	[ahlbahree**koh**keh]
banana	*plátano fruta*	[**plah**tahnoh **froo**tah]
blackberry	*mora*	[**moh**rah]
carambola	*carambola, pera china*	[kahrahm**boh**lah | **peh**rah **chee**nah]
cherry	*cereza*	[seh**reh**sah]
clementine	*mandarina*	[mahndah**reen**ah]
coconut	*coco*	[**koh**koh]
grape	*uva*	[**oo**bah]
grapefruit	*toronja*	[toh**rohn**hah]
guava	*guayaba*	[gwah**yah**bah]
kiwi	*kiwi*	[**kee**wee]
lemon	*limón*	[lee**mohn**]
lime	*lima*	[**lee**mah]
mandarine	*mandarina*	[mahndah**reen**ah]
mango	*mango*	[**mahn**goh]
melon	*melón*	[meh**lohn**]
morello	*guinda*	[**geen**dah]
nuts	*nueces*	[**nweh**sehs]
orange	*naranja*	[nah**rahn**hah]

Creature Comforts

papaya	*papaya*	[pah**pah**yah]
passionfruit	*murucuyá*	[mahrahcoo**yah**]
peach	*melocotón*	[mehlohkoh**tohn**]
peanut	*cacahuete, mani*	[kahkahwehtehs | mah**nee**]
pear	*pera*	[**peh**rah]
pineapple	*piña*	[**pee**nyah]
plantain	*plátano*	[**plah**tahnoh]
plum	*ciruela*	[seer**weh**lah]
pomelo	*toronja grande*	[toh**rohn**hah **grahn**deh]
pumpkin	*calabaza*	[kahlah**bah**sah]
raisins	*pasas*	[**pah**sahs]
raspberry	*frambuesa*	[frahm**bweh**sah]
ripe	*maduro/a*	[mah**door**oh/ah]
soursop	*guanábana*	[gwah**nah**bahnah]
strawberry	*fresas*	[**freh**sah]
tangerine	*tangerina, mandarina roja*	[tahnheh**ree**nah | mahndah**ree**nah **rroh**-hah]
unripe	*verde*	[**behr**deh]

◆ ◆ ◆

calabaza	**pumpkin**	[kahlah**bah**sah]
cacahuete	**peanut**	[kahkahwehtehs | mah**nee**]
carambola	**carambola**	[kahrahm**boh**lah]
cereza	**cherry**	[seh**reh**sah]

ciruela	**plum**	[seer**weh**lah]
coco	**coconut**	[**koh**koh]
frambuesa	**raspberry**	[frahm**bweh**sah]
fresas	**strawberry**	[**freh**sah]
guanábana	**soursop**	[gwah**nah**bahnah]
guayaba	**guava**	[gwah**yah**bah]
guinda	**morello**	[**geen**dah]
kiwi	**kiwi**	[**kee**wee]
lima	**lime**	[**lee**mah]
limón	**lemon**	[lee**mohn**]
maduro/a	**ripe**	[mah**doo**roh/ah]
mandarina	**clementine, mandarine**	[mahndah**ree**nah]
mango	**mango**	[**mahn**goh]
mani	**peanut**	[mah**nee**]
manzana	**apple**	[mahn**sah**nah]
melocotón	**peach**	[mehlohkoh**tohn**]
melón	**melon**	[meh**lohn**]
murucuyá	**passionfruit**	[mahrah**coo**yah]
naranja	**orange**	[nah**rahn**hah]
nueces	**nuts**	[**nweh**sehs]
papaya	**papaya**	[pah**pah**yah]
pasas	**raisins**	[**pah**sahs]
pera	**pear**	[**peh**rah]
piña	**pineapple**	[**pee**nyah]
plátano	**plantain**	[**plah**tahnoh]
plátano fruta	**banana**	[**plah**tahnoh **froo**tah]

tangerina	**tangerine**	[tahnheh**reen**ah]
toronja	**grapefruit**	[toh**rohn**hah]
toronja grande	**pomelo**	[toh**rohn**hah **grahn**deh]
uva	**grape**	[**oo**bah]
verde	**unripe**	[**behr**deh]

Vegetables – *Verduras*

asparagus	*espárragos*	[eh**spah**rrahgohs]
avocado	*aguacate*	[ahgwah**kah**teh]
beans	*frijoles*	[free**hoh**les]
broccoli	*brócoli, brécol*	[**broh**kohlee | breh**kohl**]
Brussels sprouts	*col de Bruxelas*	[kohl deh broo**seh**lahs]
cabbage	*col, repollo*	[kohl | rreh**poh**yoh]
cactus	*cactus, nopal*	[**kahk**toos | noh**pahl**]
carrot	*zanahoria*	[sahnah-**oh**reeah]
cauliflower	*coliflor*	[kohlee**flohr**]
celery	*apio*	[**ah**pyoh]
chickpea	*garbanzo*	[gahr**bahn**zo]
corn	*maíz*	[mah-**ees**]
cucumber	*pepino*	[peh**pee**noh]
eggplant	*berenjenas*	[behrehn**heh**nahs]
fennel	*hinojo*	[een**oh**-hoh]
garlic	*ajo*	[**ah**-hoh]
leek	*cebollino*	[sehboh**yee**noh]
lettuce	*lechuga*	[leh**choo**gah]

Creature Comforts

mushroom	*hongo,* *champiñón*	[**ohn**goh | chahmpeen**yohn**]
okra	*quimbombó,* *quiambo,* *quingambó,* *gombó*	[keembohm**boh** | **kyahm**boh | keengahm**boh** | gohm**boh**]
onion	*cebolla*	[seh**boh**yah]
pea	*judía,* *porotos*	[hoo**dee**ah | poh**roh**tohs]
potato	*papas*	[**pah**pahs]
radish	*rábanos*	[**rrah**banos]
red/hot/chili pepper	*ají*	[**ah**-hee]
snowpea	*habichuelas*	[ahbee**chweh**lahs]
spinach	*espinaca*	[ehspee**nah**kah]
squash	*calabaza*	[kahlah**bah**sah]
sweet/bell pepper	*pimiento*	[peem**yen**toh]
tomato	*tomate*	[toh**mah**teh]
turnip	*nabo*	[**nah**boh]
watercress	*berro*	[**behr**roh]
zucchini	*calabacilla,* *calabacita*	[kahlahbah**see**yah | kahlahbah**see**tah]

aguacate	**avocado**	[ahgwah**kah**teh]
ají	**red/hot/chili pepper**	[**ah**-hee]
ajo	**garlic**	[**ah**-hoh]
apio	**celery**	[**ah**pyoh]
berenjenas	**eggplant**	[behrehn**heh**nahs]

berro	**watercress**	[**beh**rroh]
brócoli *brécol*	**broccoli**	[**broh**kohlee | breh**kohl**]
cactus	**cactus**	[**kahk**toos]
calabaza	**squash**	[kahlah**bah**sah]
calabacilla, *calabacita*	**zucchini**	[kahlahbah**see**yah | kahlahbah**see**tah]
cebolla	**onion**	[seh**boh**yah]
cebollino	**leek**	[sehboh**yee**noh]
champiñón	**mushroom**	[chahmpeen**yohn**]
col	**cabbage**	[kohl]
col de Bruxelas	**Brussels sprouts**	[kohl deh broo**seh**lahs]
coliflor	**cauliflower**	[kohlee**flohr**]
espárragos	**asparagus**	[eh**spah**rrahgohs]
espinaca	**spinach**	[ehspee**nah**kah]
judía	**pea**	[hoo**dee**ah]
frijoles	**beans**	[free**hoh**les]
garbanzo	**chickpea**	[gahr**bahn**zo]
gombó	**okra**	[gohm**boh**]
habichuelas	**snowpea**	[ahbee**chweh**lahs]
hinojo	**fennel**	[ee**noh**-hoh]
hongo	**mushroom**	[**ohn**goh]
lechuga	**lettuce**	[leh**choo**gah]
maíz	**corn**	[mah-**ees**]
nabo	**turnip**	[**nah**boh]
nopal	**cactus**	[noh**pahl**]
papas	**potato**	[**pah**pahs]
pepino	**cucumber**	[peh**pee**noh]

Creature Comforts

117

pimiento	**sweet/bell pepper**	[pee**myen**toh]
porotos	**pea**	[poh**roh**tohs]
quimbombó, quiambo, quingambó	**okra**	[keembohm**boh** | **kyahm**boh | keengahm**boh**]
rábanos	**radish**	[**rrah**banos]
repollo	**cabbage**	[rreh**poh**yoh]
tomate	**tomato**	[toh**mah**teh]
zanahoria	**carrot**	[sahnah-**oh**reeah]

Meat – *Carnes*

beef	*res, vaca*	[rehs | **bah**kah]
blood sausage	*morcilla*	[mohr**see**yah]
boar	*jabalí, puerco salvaje*	[hahbah**lee** | **pweh**rkoh sahl**bah**-heh]
brains	*sesos*	[**seh**soh]
breast	*pechuga*	[peh**choo**gah]
brochette	*al pincho*	[ahl **peen**choh]
capon	*pollo de cría*	[**poh**yoh deh **kree**ah]
chicken	*pollo*	[**poh**yoh]
cubes	*cubos*	[**koo**bohs]
cutlet	*costilla*	[kohs**tee**yah]
deer	*ciervo*	[**syehr**boh]
duck	*pato*	[**pah**toh]
escalope	*escalope*	[ehskah**loh**peh]
feet	*patas*	[**pah**tahs]
filet	*filete*	[fee**leh**teh]

goat	*cabra*	[**kah**brah]
goose	*ganso/a*	[**gahn**soh/ah]
grilled meat	*asado*	[ah**sah**doh]
ground	*picado/a*	[pee**kah**doh/ah]
ham	*jamón*	[hah**mohn**]
hare	*liebre,*	[**lyeh**breh |
	mará (Argentina)	mah**rah**]
iguana	*iguana*	[ee**gwah**nah]
kid	*cabrito*	[kah**bree**toh]
kidneys	*riñones*	[rree**nyoh**nehs]
lamb	*cordero*	[kohr**deh**roh]
leg	*muslo*	[**moo**slohs]
liver	*hígado*	[**ee**gahdoh]
magret	*filete de pato*	[fee**leh**teh deh **pah**toh]
meat	*carne*	[**kahr**neh]
meat ball	*albóndigas*	[ahl**bohn**deegahs]
medium	*punto medio*	[**poon**toh **meh**dyoh]
medium rare	*rojizo*	[rroh-**hee**soh]
partridge	*perdiz*	[pehr**dees**]
pork	*puerco, cerdo*	[**pwehr**koh | **sehr**doh]
poultry	*aves*	[**ah**behs]
quail	*codorniz*	[kohdohr**nees**]
rabbit	*conejo*	[koh**neh**-hoh]
rare	*sangriento*	[sahngree**ehn**toh]
raw	*crudo*	[**kroo**doh]

Creature Comforts

ribsteak	*entrecote, solomillo*	[ehntreh**koh**teh | sohloh**mee**yoh]
sausage	*embutido, chorizo*	[ehmboo**tee**doh | choh**ree**soh]
shank	*patas, corva*	[**pah**tahs | **kohr**bah]
slice	*cortado, picado*	[kohr**tah**doh | pee**kah**doh]
smoked	*ahumado*	[ah-oo**mah**doh]
steak	*bistec, bisté*	[beef**tehk** | bees**teh**]
stuffed	*relleno*	[rreh**yeh**noh]
tartare	*tártara*	[**tahr**tahrah]
tenderloin	*filete*	[fee**leh**teh]
thigh	*muslo*	[**moos**loh]
tongue	*lengua*	[**lehn**gwah]
turkey	*guanajo, pavo*	[gwah**nah**-hoh | **pah**boh]
veal	*ternero*	[tehr**neh**roh]
venison	*venado*	[beh**nah**doh]
well done	*bien cocinado*	[byehn kohseen**ah**doh]

ahumado	**smoked**	[ah-oo**mah**doh]
al pincho	**brochette**	[ahl **peen**choh]
albóndigas	**meat ball**	[ahl**bohn**deegahs]
asado	**grilled meat**	[ah**sah**doh]
bistec, bisté	**steak**	[beef**tehk** | bees**teh**]
cabra	**goat**	[**kah**brah]
cabrito	**kid**	[kah**bree**toh]

Creature Comforts

cerdo	**pork**	[**sehr**doh]
ciervo	**deer**	[**syehr**boh]
codorniz	**quail**	[kohdohr**nees**]
conejo	**rabbit**	[koh**neh**-hoh]
cordero	**lamb**	[kohr**deh**roh]
cortado	**slice**	[kohr**tah**doh]
corva	**shank**	[**kohr**bah]
costilla	**cutlet**	[koh**stee**yah]
crudo	**raw**	[**kroo**doh]
cubos	**cubes**	[**koo**bohs]
entrecote	**ribsteak**	[ehntreh**koh**teh]
escalope	**escalope**	[ehskah**loh**peh]
filete	**filet / tenderloin**	[fee**leh**teh]
filete de pato	**magret**	[fee**leh**teh deh **pah**toh]
ganso/a	**goose**	[**gahn**soh/ah]
guanajo	**turkey**	[gwah**nah**-hoh]
hígado	**liver**	[**ee**gahdoh]
iguana	**iguana**	[ee**gwah**nah]
jabalí	**boar**	[hahbah**lee**]
jamón	**ham**	[hah**mohn**]
lengua	**tongue**	[**lehn**gwah]
liebre	**hare**	[**lyeh**breh]
morcilla	**blood sausage**	[mohr**see**yah]
muslo	**leg / thigh**	[**moo**sloh]
patas	**feet / shank**	[**pah**tahs]
pato	**duck**	[**pah**toh]

Creature Comforts

pavo	**turkey**	[**pah**boh]
pechuga	**breast**	[peh**choo**gah]
perdiz	**partridge**	[pehr**dees**]
picado/a	**ground, slice**	[pee**kah**doh/ah]
pollo	**chicken**	[**poh**yoh]
pollo de cría	**capon**	[**poh**yoh deh **kree**ah]
puerco	**pork**	[**pwehr**koh]
puerco salvaje	**boar**	[**pweh**rkoh sahl**bah**-heh]
relleno	**stuffed**	[rreh**yeh**noh]
res	**beef**	[rehs]
riñones	**kidneys**	[rreen**yoh**nehs]
sesos	**brains**	[**seh**soh]
solomillo	**ribsteak**	[sohloh**mee**yoh]
tártara	**tartare**	[**tahr**tahrah]
ternero	**veal**	[tehr**neh**roh]
vaca	**beef**	[**bah**kah]

Fish and Seafood – *Pescados y mariscos*

anchovy	*anchoas*	[ahnchoh-ahs]
bass	*bar*	[bahr]
clams	*cobo, caracol*	[**koh**boh | kahrah**kohl**]
cod	*bacalao*	[bahkah**lah**-oh]
crab	*cangrejo*	[kahn**greh**-hoh]
eel	*anguila*	[ahn**gee**lah]
escargot, snails	*cobo, caracol*	[**koh**boh | kahrah**kohl**]

filet	*filete*	[fee**leh**teh]
(fish) steak	*rodaja*	[rroh**dah**-hah]
hake	*merluza*	[mehr**loo**sah]
herring	*arenque*	[ah**rehn**keh]
lobster	*langosta grande, cobrajo*	[lahn**goh**stah **grahn**deh | koh**brah**-hoh]
mullet	*rabi rubia, huachinango*	[rahbee**rroo**byah | wachee**nahng**goh]
octopus	*pulpo pequeño, pulpo*	[**pool**poh peh**keh**nyoh | **pool**poh]
oysters	*ostras*	[**oh**strahs]
ray	*raya*	[**rrah**yah]
rock lobster	*langosta*	[lahn**goh**stah]
salmon	*salmón*	[sahl**mohn**]
sardines	*sardinas*	[sahr**dee**nahs]
scallops	*pechina*	[peh**chee**nah]
scampi	*langostín, langostino*	[lahngoh**steen** | lahngoh**stee**noh]
sea urchin	*erizo*	[eh**ree**soh]
shark	*tiburón*	[teeboo**rohn**]
shrimps	*camarones, gambas*	[kahmah**rohn**nehs | **gahm**bahs]
smoked salmon	*salmón ahumado*	[sahl**mohn** ah-oo**mah**doh]
sole	*lenguado*	[lehng**wah**doh]
squid	*calamar*	[kahlah**mahr**]
striped bass	*lobo de mar*	[**loh**boh deh mahr]
swordfish	*espadón*	[ehspah**dohn**]

trout	*trucha*	[**troo**chah]
tuna	*atún*	[ah**toon**]
turbot	*turbo*	[**toor**boh]
whiting	*merlán*	[mehr**lahn**]

anchoas	**anchovy**	[ahnchoh-ahs]
anguila	**eel**	[ahn**gee**lah]
arenque	**herring**	[ah**rehn**keh]
atún	**tuna**	[ah**toon**]
bacalao	**cod**	[bahkah**lah**-oh]
bar	**bass**	[bahr]
calamar	**squid**	[kahlah**mahr**]
cangrejo	**crab**	[kahn**greh**-hoh]
camarones	**shrimps**	[kahmah**rohn**ehs]
cobo	**clams**	[**koh**boh]
cobrajo	**lobster**	[koh**brah**-hoh]
caracol	**escargot, snails**	[kahrah**kohl**]
erizo	**sea urchin**	[eh**ree**soh]
espadón	**swordfish**	[ehspah**dohn**]
filete	**filet**	[fee**leh**teh]
gambas	**shrimps**	[**gahm**bahs]
huachinango	**mullet**	[wachee**nahn**goh]
langosta	**rock lobster**	[lahn**goh**stah]
langosta grande	**lobster**	[lahn**goh**stah **grahn**deh]

langostín, *langostino*	**scampi**	[lahngoh**steen** | lahngohstee**noh**]
lenguado	**sole**	[leh**ngwah**doh]
lobo de mar	**striped bass**	[**loh**boh deh mahr]
merlán	**whiting**	[mehr**lahn**]
merluza	**hake**	[mehr**loo**sah]
ostras	**oysters**	[**oh**strahs]
petchina	**scallops**	[peh**chee**nah]
pulpo, *pulpo pequeño*	**octopus**	[**pool**poh | **pool**poh peh**keh**nyoh]
rabi rubia	**mullet**	[rahbeer**roo**byah]
raya	**ray**	[**rrah**yah]
rodaja	**(fish) steak**	[rroh**dah**-hah]
salmón	**salmon**	[sahl**mohn**]
salmón ahumado	**smoked salmon**	[sahl**mohn** ah-oo**mahd**oh]
sardinas	**sardines**	[sahr**dee**nahs]
tiburón	**shark**	[teeboo**rohn**]
trucha	**trout**	[**troo**chah]
turbo	**turbot**	[**toor**boh]

Desserts – *Postres*

cake	*pastel, cake*	[pahstehl | **keh**ee]
caramel	*caramelo*	[kahrah**meh**loh]
chocolate	*chocolate*	[chohkoh**lah**teh]
chocolate mousse	*mousse de chocolate*	[moos deh chohkoh**lah**teh]

Creature Comforts

125

custard	*crema postre* *natillas*	[**kreh**mah **poh**streh | **nah**teeyahs]
flan	*flan*	[flahn]
ice cream	*helado*	[eh**lah**doh]
meringue	*merengue*	[meh**rehn**geh]
pie	*torta, pastel*	[**tohr**tah | pah**stehl**]
sorbet	*sorbeto, sorbete*	[sohr**beh**toh | sohr**beh**teh]
vanilla	*vainilla*	[bah-ee**nee**yah]

◆ ◆ ◆

caramelo	**caramel**	[kahrah**meh**loh]
cake	**cake**	[**keh**ee]
chocolate	**chocolate**	[chohkoh**lah**teh]
crema postre	**custard**	[**kreh**mah **poh**streh]
flan	**flan**	[flahn]
pastel	**cake**	[pah**stehl**]
helado	**ice cream**	[eh**lah**doh]
merengue	**meringue**	[meh**rehn**geh]
mousse de chocolate	**chocolate mousse**	[moos deh chohkoh**lah**teh]
sorbeto, sorbete	**sorbet**	[sohr**beh**toh | sohr**beh**teh]
torta	**pie**	[**tohr**tah]
vainilla	**vanilla**	[bah-ee**nee**yah]

Special Events – *Diversión*

ballet	*ballet*	[bah**leh**]
baseball	*béisbol, pelota*	[**beh**-eesbohl | peh**loh**tah]
bullfight	*tauromaquia*	[tahooroh**mah**keeah]
bullfighter	*torero*	[toh**reh**roh]
concert	*concierto*	[kohns**yehr**toh]
folk dance	*danza folklórica*	[**dahn**sah fohlk**loh**reekah]
folklore	*folklore*	[fohlk**lohr**]
hockey	*hockey*	[**oh**kee]
intermission	*entreacto*	[ehntreh**ahk**toh]
movie theatre	*cine*	[**see**neh]
opera	*ópera*	[**oh**pehrah]
program	*programa*	[proh**grah**mah]
reserved seat	*asiento reservado*	[ah**syehn**toh rehsehr**vah**doh]
seat	*asiento*	[ah**syehn**toh]
show	*espectáculo*	[ehspehk**tah**kooloh]
soccer	*fútbol*	[**foot**bohl]
theatre	*teatro*	[the-**ah**troh]
ticket counter, ticket office	*taquilla*	[tah**kee**yah]

The least expensive seats.
Los asientos más baratos
[lohs ah**syehn**tohs mahs bah**rah**tohs]

Creature Comforts

The best seats.
Los mejores asientos
[lohs meh-**hoh**rehs ah**syehn**tohs]

I would like... seats.
Quisiera... asientos.
[kee**syeh**rah ... ah**syehn**tohs]

Are seats still available for...?
¿Quedan asientos para...?
[**keh**dahn ah**syehn**tohs **pah**rah]

What days is... showing?
¿Qué día presentan...?
[keh **dee**ah preh**sehn**tahn...]

Is it in the original version?
¿Es en versión original?
[ehs ehn behr**syohn** ohreehee**nahl**]

Is it subtitled?
¿Está subtitulado?
[eh**stah** soobteetoo**lah**doh]

Nightlife – *La vida nocturna*

English	Spanish	Pronunciation
bar	*bar*	[bahr]
bartender	*barman, camarero*	[**bahr**mahn | cahmah**reh**roh]
cover charge ($)	*entrada*	[ehn**trah**dah]
dance	*baile*	[**bah**-eeleh]

dance floor	*pista, plataforma (de baile)*	[**pee**stah | plahtah**fohr**mah | deh **bah**-eeleh]
discotheque	*discoteca*	[deeskoh**teh**kah]
drink	*consumo*	[kohn**soo**moh]
gay bar	*bar de gays*	[bahr deh **geh**-ees]
the gay scene	*el ambiente gay*	[ahm**byehn**teh **geh**-ee]
jazz	*jazz*	[yahs | jahs]
lesbian bar	*bar de lesbianas*	[bahr deh lehz**byah**nahs]
live music	*música en vivo*	[**moo**seekah ehn **bee**boh]
musician	*músico*	[**moo**seekoh]
nightclub	*cabaré, dáncing*	[kahbah**reh** | **dahn**seen]
party	*fiesta*	[**fyeh**stah]
singer	*cantante*	[kahn**tahn**teh]
strip-tease	*strip-tease*	[ehstreep**tees**]
transvestite	*travesti*	[trahbeh**stee**]
a drink / a glass	*un trago*	[oon **trah**goh]
alcohol	*alcohol*	[ahl**kohl**]
aperitif	*aperitivo*	[ahpehree**tee**boh]
beer	*cerveza*	[sehr**beh**sah]
coffee chaser	*digestivo*	[deeheh**stee**boh]
imported drink	*bebida importada*	[beh**bee**dah eempohr**tah**dah]
local drink	*bebida nacional*	[beh**bee**dah nahsyoh**nahl**]

Creature Comforts

mineral water	*agua mineral*	[**ahg**wah meeneh**rahl**]
orange juice	*jugo de naranja*	[**hoo**goh deh nah**rahn**-ha]
soda water	*soda*	[**soh**dah]
sparkling mineral water	*agua mineral gaseosa*	[**ahg**wah meeneh-**rahl** gahseh-**oh**sah]
tequila	*tequila*	[teh**kee**lah]
vermouth	*vermú*	[behr**moo**]
wine	*vino*	[**bee**noh]

Meeting People - *Encuentros*

affectionate	*cariñoso*	[kahreenyohsoh]
alone	*solo/a*	[**soh**loh/ah]
beautiful	*bonito/a, guapo/a, hermoso/a*	[boh**nee**toh/ah | g**wah**poh/ah | ehr**moh**soh/ah]
boy	*chico, muchacho*	[**chee**koh | moo**chah**choh]
charming	*encantador/a*	[ehnkahntah**dohr**/ah]
cheers (to toast)	*¡salud!*	[sah**lood**]
compliment	*complimentos*	[kohmplee**mehn**tohs]
conquest	*conquista*	[kohn**kee**stah]
couple	*pareja*	[pah**reh**-hah]
cute	*bonito/a, hermoso/a*	[boh**nee**toh/ah | ehr**moh**soh/ah]
date	*cita*	[**see**tah]
daughter	*chica, muchacha*	[**chee**kah | moo**chah**chah]
discreet	*discreto/a*	[dees**kreh**toh/ah]

divorced	*divorciado/a*	[deebohr**syah**doh/ah]
drunk	*borracho, ebrio,* *curda*	[boh**rrah**choh | **ehb**reeoh | **koor**dah]
faithful	*fiel*	[fyehl]
to flirt	*ligar*	[lee**gahr**]
gay	*gay,* *homosexual*	[**geh**-ee | ohmohsehk**swahl**]
girl	*chica,* *muchacha*	[**chee**kah | moo**chah**chah]
to have a drink	*tomar (darse)* *un trago*	[toh**mahr** | **dahr**seh | oon **trah**goh]
invitation	*invitación*	[eenbeetah**syohn**]
to invite	*invitar*	[eenbee**tahr**]
jealous	*celoso/a*	[seh**loh**soh/ah]
macho	*macho*	[**mah**choh]
man	*hombre*	[**ohm**breh]
married	*casado/a*	[kah**sah**doh/ah]
nice	*simpático/a*	[seem**pah**teekoh/ah]
old	*viejo/a*	[**byeh**-hoh/ah]
personality	*personalidad*	[pehrsohnahlee**dah**]
play pool	*jugar al billar*	[hoo**gahr** ahl bee**yahr**]
pleased to meet you	*encantado/a*	[ehnkahntah**doh**/ah]
pretty	*bonito/a, lindo/a*	[boh**nee**toh/ah | **leen**doh/ah]
safe sex	*sexo seguro*	[**sehk**soh seh**goo**roh]
separated	*separado/a*	[sehpah**rah**doh/ah]
sexy	*sexy*	[**sehk**see]
single	*soltero/a*	[sohl**teh**roh/ah]

Creature Comforts

small	*pequeño/a*	[peh**keh**nyoh/ah]
tall	*grande*	[**grahn**deh]
tired	*fatigado/a*	[fahtee**gah**doh/ah]
ugly	*feo/a*	[**feh**-oh/ah]
woman	*mujer*	[moo**her**]
young	*joven*	[**hoh**behn]

How are you?
¿Cómo está usted?
[**koh**moh eh**stah** oo**steh**]

Fine, and you?
¿Muy bien, y usted?
[mwee byehn, ee oo**steh**]

I would like to introduce you to...
Le presento a...
[leh preh**sehn**toh ah...]

Could you introduce me to this young lady?
¿Podría usted presentarme a esa muchacha?
[poh**dree**ah oo**steh** prehsehn**tahr**meh ah **eh**sah moo**chah**chah]

What time do most people get here?
¿A qué hora viene la mayoría de las personas?
[ah keh **oh**rah **byeh**neh la mayoh**ree**ah deh lahs pehr**soh**nahs]

What time is the show?
¿A qué hora es el espectáculo?
[ah keh ohrah ehs ehl ehspehk**tah**kooloh]

Hello, my name is...
Buenas noches, me llamo...
[**bweh**nahs **noh**chehs, meh **yah**moh...]

Do you like this music?
¿Te gusta esa música?
[teh **goo**stah **eh**sah **moo**seekah]

I am straight.
Soy heterosexual.
[soy ehtehrohsehk**swahl**]

I am gay.
Soy gay, homo.
[soy **geh**-ee | **oh**moh]

I am a lesbian.
Soy lesbiana.
[soy lehz**byah**nah]

I am bisexual.
Soy bisexual.
[soy beesehk**swahl**]

Is that your friend over there?
¿Aquél es tu amigo?
[ah**kehl** ehs too ah**mee**goh]

Which one?	¿Cuál?	[kwahl]
The blonde	el rubio	[ehl **rroo**byoh]
The redhead	el pelirrojo	[ehl pehlee**rroh**-hoh]
The brunette	el moreno	[ehl moh**reh**noh]

Creature Comforts

Would you like a drink?
¿Tomas un trago?
[**toh**mahs oon trahgoh]

What are you having?
¿Qué vas a tomar?
[keh bahs ah toh**mahr**]

What country do you come from?
¿De qué país vienes tú?
[deh keh pah-**ees byeh**nehs too]

Are you here on vacation or for work?
¿Estás aquí de vacaciones o por trabajo?
[eh**stahs** ahkee deh bahkah**syoh**nehs oh pohr trah**bah**-hoh]

What do you do in life?
¿Qué haces en la vida?
[keh **ah**sehs ehn lah **vee**dah]

Have you been living here long?
¿Vives aquí desde hace tiempo?
[**bee**behs ah**kee deh**sdeh **ah**seh **tyehm**poh]

Does your family live here too?
¿Tu familia vive también aquí?
[too fah**mee**lyah **bee**beh tahm**byehn** ah**kee**]

Do you have brothers and sisters?
¿Tienes hermanos?
[**tyeh**nehs ehr**mah**nohs]

Do you want to dance?
¿Vienes a bailar?
[**byeh**nehs ah baheel**ahr**]

Let's find a quiet spot to talk.
Busquemos un lugar tranquilo para charlar.
[boo**skeh**mohs oon loo**gahr** trahn**keel**oh **pah**rah chahr**lahr**]

You are very cute.
Eres muy lindo/a, bonito/a, hermoso/a.
[**eh**rehs mwee **leen**doh/ah | boh**nee**to/ah | hehr**moh**soh/ah]

Do you have a boyfriend / girlfriend?
¿Tienes un amigo/a?
[**tyeh**nehs oon ah**mee**goh/ah]

Too bad!
¡Que lástima!
[keh **lah**steemah]

Do you like men / women?
¿Te gustan los hombres (las mujeres)?
[teh **goo**stahn lohs **ohm**brehs | lahs moo**heh**-rehs]

Do you have children?
¿Tienes hijos?
[**tyeh**nehs **ee**hohs]

Could we meet again tomorrow night?
¿Podemos volver a vernos mañana por la noche?
[poh**deh**mohs bohl**behr** ah **behr**nohs mah**nyah**nah pohr lah **noh**cheh]

Creature Comforts

When can I see you again?
¿Cuándo podemos volver a vernos?
[**kwahn**doh poh**deh**mohs bohl**behr** ah **behr**nohs]

I would like to invite you to dinner tomorrow night.
Me gustaría invitarte a comer mañana por la noche.
[meh goostah**ree**ah eembee**tahr**teh ah koh**mehr** mah**nyah**nah pohr lah **noh**cheh]

Would you like to come to my place?
¿Vienes a mi casa?
[**byeh**nehs ah mee **kah**sah]

Could we go to your place?
¿Podemos ir a tu casa?
[poh**deh**mohs eer ah too **kah**sah]

I had an excellent evening with you.
He pasado una excelente noche contigo.
[eh pah**sah**doh **oo**nah ehkseh**lehn**teh **noh**cheh kohn**tee**goh]

SHOPPING – *IR DE COMPRAS*

What time do the stores open?
¿A qué hora abren las tiendas?
[ah keh **oh**rah **ah**brehn lahs **tyehn**dahs]

What time do the stores close?
¿A qué hora cierran las tiendas?
[ah keh **oh**rah **syeh**rrahn lahs **tyehn**dahs]

Are the stores open today?
¿Las tiendas están abiertas hoy?
[lahs **tyehn**dahs ehs**tahn** ah**byehr**tahs **oh**-ee]

What time do you close?
¿A qué hora cierra usted?
[ah keh **oh**rah **syeh**rrah oos**teh**]

What time do you open tomorrow?
¿A qué hora abre usted mañana?
[ah keh **oh**rah **ah**breh oos**teh** mah**nyah**nah]

Do you have other stores?
¿Tiene usted otras sucursales?
[**tyeh**neh oos**teh oh**trahs sookoor**sah**lehs]

What is the price?
¿Cuál es el precio?
[kwahl ehs ehl **preh**syoh]

How much does this cost?
¿Eso cuánto es (cuesta)?
[**eh**soh **kwahn**toh ehs | **kweh**stah]

Do you have any less expensive ones?
¿Tiene más baratos?
[**tyeh**neh mahs bah**rah**tohs]

I am looking for a... store.
Busco una tienda de
[**boo**skoh **oo**nah **tyehn**dah deh...]

Where is the closest supermarket?
¿Dónde se encuentra el supermercado más cercano?
[**dohn**deh seh ehn**kwehn**trah ehl soopehrmehr**kah**doh mahs sehr**kah**noh]

clothing	*ropas, vestidos*	[**rroh**pahs | beh**stee**dohs]
gift	*regalo*	[reh**gah**loh]
market	*mercado*	[mehr**kah**doh]
postcard	*tarjeta postal*	[tahr**heh**tah poh**stahl**]
shopping mall	*centro comercial*	[**sehn**troh kohmehr**syahl**]
stamps	*sellos, estampillas*	[**seh**yohs | ehstahm**pee**yahs]
store / boutique	*tienda*	[**tyehn**dah]

Different stores – *Varias tiendas*

beauty products	*productos de belleza*	[proh**dook**tohs deh beh**yeh**sah]
bookstore	*librería*	[leebreh**ree**ah]
book	*libro*	[**lee**broh]
coffee table book	*libro con ilustraciones*	[**lee**broh kohn ee-loostrah**syoh**nehs]
dictionary	*diccionario*	[deeksyoh**nah**reeoh]
guide	*guía*	[**gee**ah]
literature	*literatura*	[leetehrah**too**rah]
magazines	*revistas*	[reh**bee**stahs]
map	*mapa*	[**mah**pah]
more detailed map	*mapa más preciso*	[**mah**pah mahs preh**see**soh]
newspapers	*diarios, periódicos*	[**dyah**reeohs | pehree**oh**deekohs]
poetry	*poesía*	[poh-eh**see**ah]

Creature Comforts

138

| **road atlas** | *libro de carreteras* | [**lee**broh deh kahrreh**teh**rahs] |

| **street atlas** | *repertorio de calles* | [rehpehr**toh**reeoh deh **kah**yehs] |

Do you have books in English?
¿Tiene libros en inglés?
[**tyeh**neh **lee**brohs ehn een**glehs**]

| **butcher** | *carnicería* | [kahrneeseh**ree**ah] |

| **computer equipment** | *equipo de informática* | [eh**kee**poh deh eenfohr**mah**teekah] |

Do you do repairs?
¿Hace reparaciones?
[**ah**seh rehpahrah**syoh**nehs]

How / Where can I log on to the Internet?
¿Cómo (dónde) puedo conectarme con Internet?
[**koh**moh | **dohn**deh | **pweh**doh kohnehk**tahr**meh kohn eentehr**neht**]

| **dry cleaner** | *lavado en seco* | [lah**bah**doh ehn **seh**koh] |

Could you wash and iron this shirt for tomorrow?
¿Puede lavar y planchar esta camisa para mañana?
[**pweh**deh lah**bahr** ee plahn**chahr** **ehs**tah kah**mee**sah **pah**rah mah**nyah**nah]

| **electronic equipment** | *aparatos electrónicos* | [ahpah**rah**tohs ehlehk**troh**neekohs] |

I would like a new battery for...
Quisiera una pila nueva para...
[kee**syeh**rah **oo**nah **pee**lah **nweh**bah **pah**rah]

eye doctor *oculista* [ohkoo**lee**stah]

I have broken my glasses.
Rompí mis gafas (espejuelos, lentes).
[rohm**pee** mees **gah**fahs | ehspeh-**hweh**lohs | **lehn**tehs]

I would like to replace my glasses.
Quisiera cambiar mis espejuelos (gafas).
[kee**syeh**rah kahm**byahr** mees ehspeh-**hweh**lohs | **gah**fahs]

I have lost my glasses.
Perdí mis espejuelos (gafas).
[pehr**dee** mees ehspeh-**hweh**lohs | **gah**fahs]

I have lost my contact lenses.
Perdí mis lentes de contacto.
[pehr**dee** mees **lehn**tehs deh kohn**tahk**toh]

Here is my prescription.
Esta es mi receta.
[**eh**stah ehs mee reh**seh**tah]

I should have a new eye exam.
Debo hacerme un nuevo examen de la vista.
[**deh**boh ah**sehr**meh oon **nweh**boh ehk**sah**mehn deh lah **bee**stah]

fish store *pescadería* [pehskahdeh**ree**ah]

hairdresser / barber *peluquero* [pehloo**keh**roh]

handicraft market	mercado de artesanía	[mehr**kah**doh deh ahrtehsah**nee**ah]
handicrafts	artesanía	[ahrtehsah**nee**ah]
hardware store	quincallería, ferretería	[keenkahyeh**ree**ah | fehrrehteh**ree**ah]
health foods	alimentos naturales	[ahlee**mehn**tohs nahtoo**rah**lehs]
laundromat	lavandería	[lahbahndeh**ree**ah]
music store	tienda de discos	[**tyehn**dah deh **dee**skohs]

Do you have a disk by...?
¿Tiene un disco de ...
[**tyeh**neh oon **dee**skoh deh]

What is the latest disk by...?
¿Cuál es el disco más reciente de...?
[kwahl ehs ehl **dee**skoh mahs rreh**syehn**teh deh]

Could you play it for me?
¿Lo puedo escuchar?
[loh **pweh**doh ehskoo**chahr**]

Could you tell me who sings...?
¿Puede decirme quién canta   ?
[**pweh**deh deh**seer**meh kyehn **kahn**tah]

Do you have another disk by...?
¿Tiene otro disco de...?
[**tyeh**neh **oh**troh **dee**skoh deh]

Creature Comforts

pharmacy	*farmacia*	[fahr**mah**syah]
photography equipment	*equipo de fotografía*	[eh**kee**poh deh fohtohgrah**fee**ah]
public market	*mercado público*	[mehr**kah**doh **poo**bleekoh]
sports equipment	*equipo deportivo*	[eh**kee**poh dehpohr**tee**boh]
supermarket	*mercado de alimentos, supermercado*	[mehr**kah**doh deh ahlee**mehn**tohs | soopehrmehr**kah**doh]
toys	*juegos*	[hoo**eh**gohs]
travel agent	*agente de viaje*	[ah-**hehn**teh deh byah-**hehs**]

I would like to change my return date.
Quisiera modificar mi fecha de regreso.
[kees**yeh**rah mohdeefee**kahr** mee **feh**chah deh rreh**greh**soh]

I would like to buy a ticket for...
Quisiera comprar un billete para...
[kees**yeh**rah kohm**prahr** oon bee**yeh**teh **pah**rah]

Could you give me a discount?
¿Puede hacerme un mejor precio?
[**pweh**deh ah**sehr**meh oon meh-**hor preh**syoh]

Do you take credit cards?
¿Acepta tarjetas de crédito?
[ah**sehp**tah tahr**heh**tahs deh **kreh**deetoh]

children's clothing	*ropa para niños*	[**rroh**pah **pah**rah **nee**nyohs]
men's clothing	*ropa para hombres*	[**rroh**pah **pah**rah **ohmb**rehs]
sportswear	*ropa deportiva*	[**rroh**pah dehpohr**tee**bah]
women's clothing	*ropa para mujeres*	[**rroh**pah **pah**rah moo-**heh**rehs]
anorak	*impermeable, chubasquero*	[eempehrmeh-**ah**bleh | choobah**skeh**roh]
bathing suit	*traje de baño, bañador, trusa (Cuba)*	[**trah**-heh deh **bah**nyoh | bahnyah**dohr** | **troo**sah]
bathrobe	*bata de casa, de cuarto, de levantar*	[**bah**tah deh **kah**sah | deh **kwahr**toh | deh lehbahn**tahr**]
belt	*cinto*	[**seen**toh]
boxer shorts	*calzoncillo, calzones*	[kahlsohn**see**yohs | kahl**sohn**ehs]
bra	*ajustador, sosten*	[ah-hoostah**dohr** | sohs**tehn**]
cap	*gorra*	[**goh**rrah]
coat	*abrigo*	[ah**bree**goh]
dress	*vestido*	[beh**stee**doh]
hat	*sombrero*	[sohm**breh**roh]
jacket	*chaquetón*	[chahkeh**tohn**]

jeans	jeans, vaqueros, tejanos, pitusa	[yeens | bah**keh**-rohs | teh-**hah**-nohs | pee**too**sah]
men's suit jacket	chaqueta	[chah**keh**tah]
pants	pantalón	[pahntah**lohn**]
pullover	jersey, pulóver	[**yehr**see | poo**loh**behr]
shirt	camisa	[kah**mee**sah]
shoes	zapatos	[sah**pah**tohs]
shorts	pantalones cortos	[pahntah**loh**nehs **kohr**tohs]
skirt	saya, falda, pollera (Panamá)	[**sah**yah | **fahl**dah | poh**yeh**rah]
socks	medias	[**meh**dyahs]
suit	traje	[**trah**-heh]
sweater	suéter, jersey	[**sweh**tehr | **yehr**see]
tie	corbata	[kohr**bah**tah]
t-shirt	camiseta, pulover	[kahmee**sehh**tah | poo**loh**vehr]
underpants	blúmer, panti, calzones	[**bloo**mehr | **pahn**tee | kahl**soh**nehs]
underwear	ropa interior	[**roh**pah eentehree**ohr**]
windbreaker	impermeable	[eempehrmeh-**ah**bleh]
women's suit jacket	traje, combinación	[**trah**-heh | kohm-beenah**syohn**]

Could I try it on?
¿me lo puedo probar?
[meh loh **pweh**doh proh**bahr**]

Could I try on a larger size?
¿Puedo probarme una talla más grande?
[**pweh**doh proh**bahr**meh **oo**nah **tah**yah mahs **grahn**dehs]

Could I try on a smaller size?
¿Puedo probarme una talla más pequeña?
[**pweh**doh proh**bahr**meh **oo**nah **tah**yah mahs peh**keh**nyah]

Do you sew hems? Do you do alterations?
¿Hace los bordes? ¿los retoques?
[**ah**seh lohs **bohr**dehs | lohs rreh**toh**kehs]

Do I have to pay for alterations?
¿Hay que pagar por los retoques?
[**ah**-ee keh pah**gahr** pohr lohs rreh**toh**kehs]

When will it be ready?
¿Para cuándo estará listo?
[**pah**rah **kwahn**doh ehstah**rah lee**stoh]

Do you have any... ones?
¿Tiene más...?
[**tyeh**neh mahs]

bigger	*grandes*	[**grahn**dehs]
darker	*oscuros*	[oh**skoo**rohs]
lighter	*claros*	[**klah**rohs |
	ligeros	lee-**heh**rohs]

Creature Comforts

more economical	*económicos*	[ehkoh**noh**meekohs]
roomier	*amplios*	[**ahm**plyohs]
simpler	*simples*	[**seem**plehs]
smaller	*pequeños*	[peh**keh**nyohs]
softer	*suaves*	[**swah**behs]
tighter	*estrechos*	[ehs**treh**chohs]
wider	*anchos*	[**ahn**chohs]

Fabrics – *Telas*

acrylic	*acrílico*	[ah**kree**leekoh]
cotton	*algodón*	[ahlgoh**dohn**]
linen	*lino, hilo*	[**lee**noh │ **ee**loh]
polyester	*poliester*	[pohlee-**ehs**tehr]
rayon	*rayón (seda artificial)*	[rrah**yohn** (**seh**dah ahrteefees**yahl**)]
silk	*seda*	[**seh**dah]
wool	*lana*	[**lah**nah]

What material is it made of?
¿De qué material está hecho?
[deh keh mahtehree**ahl** ehs**tah eh**choh]

Is it one hundred percent (100%) cotton?
¿Es algodón 100%?
[ehs ahlgoh**dohn** syehn pohr **syehn**toh]

PROFESSIONAL LIFE –
VIDA PROFESIONAL

I would like to introduce you to...	*Le presento a...*	[leh preh**sehn**toh ah]
Pleased to meet you.	*Encantado/a*	[ehnkahn**tah**doh/ah]

I would like to meet with the director.
Me gustaría tener una cita con el director.
[meh goostah**ree**ah teh**nehr oo**nah **see**tah kohn ehl deerehk**tohr**]

Could I have the name of the director?
¿Puede darme el nombre del director?
[**pweh**deh **dahr**meh ehl **nohm**breh dehl deerehk**tohr**]

Could I have the name of the person in charge...?
¿Puede darme el nombre de la persona responsable...?
[**pweh**deh **dahr**meh ehl **nohm**breh deh lah pehr**soh**nah rrehspohn**sah**bleh]

of accounting	*de la contabilidad*	[deh lah kohn-tahbeelee**dahd**]
of exports	*de las exportaciones*	[deh lahs ehks-pohrtah**syoh**nehs]
of human resources	*del personal*	[dehl pehrsoh**nahl**]
of imports	*de las importaciones*	[deh lahs eem-pohrtah**syoh**nehs]
of marketing	*del marketing*	[dehl **mahr**kehteen]
of purchasing	*de las compras*	[lahs **kohm**prahs]
of sales	*de las ventas*	[deh lahs **behn**tahs]

It is urgent.　　　　　*Es urgente*　　　[ehs oor**hehn**teh]

I am..., from the... company.
Soy..., de la sociedad...
[soy... deh lah sohsyeh**dah**...]

She is not here at the moment.
Ella no está aquí en este momento.
[**eh**yah noh eh**stah** ah**kee** ehn **eh**steh moh**mehn**toh]

She has gone out.
Ella salió.
[**eh**yah sahl**yoh**]

When will she be back?
¿Cuándo estará de regreso?
[**kwahn**doh ehstah**rah** deh reh**greh**soh]

Could you ask her/him to call me?
¿Puede decirle que me llame?
[**pweh**deh deh**seer**leh keh meh **yah**meh]

I am stopping over in Mexico City for three days.
Estoy de pasada en México por tres días.
[eh**stoy** deh pah**sah**dah ehn **meh**-heekoh pohr trehs **dee**as]

I am at the Hotel... You can reach me at..., room...
Estoy en el hotel... Puede encontrarme en..., habitación...
[eh**stoy** ehn ehl oh**tehl**... **Pweh**deh ehnkohn**trahr**meh ehn... | ahbeetah**syohn**...]

I would like to meet with you briefly to show you our new product.

Me gustaría encontrarme un momento con usted para presentarle nuestro producto.

[meh goostah**ree**ah ehnkohn**trahr**meh oon moh**mehn**toh kohn oo**steh pah**rah prehsehn**tahr**leh **nweh**stroh prohd**ook**toh]

I would like to meet with you briefly to discuss a project.

Me gustaría encontrarle un momento para discutir sobre un proyecto.

[meh goostah**ree**ah ehnkohn**trahr**leh oon moh**mehn**toh **pah**rah deeskooo**teer soh**breh oon proh**yehk**toh]

We are looking for a distributor for...

Buscamos un distribuidor para...

[boo**skah**mohs oon deestreebwee**dohr pah**rah]

We would like to import your product, the...

Nos gustaría importar su producto, el...

[nohs goostah**ree**a eempohr**tahr** soo prohd**ook**toh, ehl]

Professions – *Las profesiones*

accountant	*contador/a*	[kohntah**dohr**/ah]
administator	*administrador/a*	[ahdmee-neestrah**dohr**/ah]
architect	*arquitecto*	[ahrkee**tehk**toh/ah]
artist	*artista*	[ahr**tee**stah]
athlete	*atleta*	[aht**leh**tah]
biologist	*biólogo/a*	[**byoh**lohgoh/ah]
bookseller	*librero/a*	[lee**breh**roh/ah]
chef	*cocinero/a*	[kohsee**neh**roh/ah]
civil servant	*funcionario*	[foonsyoh**nah**reeoh]
computer expert	*informático/a*	[eenfohr**mah**teekoh/ah]
dentist	*dentista*	[dehn**tee**stah]
designer	*diseñador*	[deesehnyah**dohr**]
dietician	*dietetista*	[dyehteh**tis**tah]
director	*director/a*	[deerehk**tohr**/ah]
doctor	*médico/a*	[**meh**deekoh/ah]
editor	*editor/a*	[ehdee**tohr**/ah]
engineer	*ingeniero*	[eeneh**nyeh**roh]
flight attendant	*tripulante*	[treepoo**lahn**teh]
graphic artist	*grafista*	[grah**fee**stah]
hairdresser	*peluquero/a*	[pehloo**keh**roh/ah]
journalist	*periodista*	[pehreeoh**dee**stah]
lawyer	*abogado/a*	[ahboh**gah**doh/ah]
mechanic	*mecánico/a*	[meh**kah**neekoh/ah]
military serviceman	*militar*	[meelee**tahr**]

musician	*músico*	[**moo**seekoh]
nurse	*enfermero/a*	[ehnfehr**meh**roh/ah]
photographer	*fotógrafo/a*	[foh**toh**grahfoh/ah]
pilot	*piloto*	[pee**loh**toh]
professor / teacher	*profesor/a*	[prohfeh**sohr**/ah]
psychologist	*psicólogo/a*	[see**koh**lohgoh/ah]
publisher	*editor/a*	[ehdee**tohr**/ah]
salesperson	*vendedor/a*	[behndeh**dohr**/ah]
secretary	*secretario/a*	[sehkreh**tah**reeoh/ah]
student	*estudiante*	[ehstoo**dyahn**teh]
technician	*técnico/a*	[**tehk**neekoh/ah]
tour guide	*guía acompañante*	[**gee**ah ahkohm-pah**nyahn**teh]
travel agent	*agente de viajes*	[ah-**hehn**teh deh **byah**-hehs]
unemployed	*estoy sin trabajo, parado/a*	[eh**stoy** seen trah**bah**-hoh | pah**rah**doh/ah]
urban planner	*urbanista*	[oorbah**nee**stah]
waiter	*camarero/a*	[kahmah**reh**roh/ah]
worker	*obrero/a*	[oh**breh**roh/ah]
writer	*escritor/a*	[ehskree**tohr**/ah]

construction	*de la construcción*	[deh lah kohnstrook**syohn**]
design	*del diseño*	[dehl dee**seh**nyoh]
education	*de la educación*	[deh lah ehdookah**syohn**]
electricity	*de la electricidad*	[deh lah ehlehktreesee**dah**]
food service	*de la restauración*	[deh lah rehstah-oorah**syohn**]
health	*de la salud*	[deh lah sah**lood**]
manufacturing	*de la manufactura*	[deh lah mahnoofahk**too**rah]
media	*de las comunicaciónes*	[deh lahs kohmoo-neekah**syoh**nehs]
music	*de la música*	[deh lah **moo**seekah]
public sector	*del público*	[dehl **poo**bleekoh]
publishing	*de la edición*	[deh lah ehdee**syohn**]
show business	*del espectáculo*	[dehl ehspehk**tah**kooloh]
sport	*del deporte*	[dehl deh**pohr**teh]
telecommunications	*de las telecomunicaciones*	[deh lahs tehlehkoh-mooneekah**syoh**nehs]
travel	*de los viajes*	[deh lohs **byah**-hehs]

Human Relations

Studies – *Estudios*

accounting	*contabilidad*	[kohntahbeelee**dah**]
administration	*administración*	[ahdmee-neestrah**syohn**]
architecture	*arquitectura*	[ahrkeetehk**too**rah]
art	*arte*	[**ahr**teh]
biology	*biología*	[byohloh-**hee**ah]
computer science	*informática*	[eenfohr**mah**teekah]
engineering	*ingeniería*	[eenhehnyeh**ree**ah]
environmental studies	*medio ambiente*	[**meh**dyoh ahm**byehn**teh]
geography	*geografía*	[heh-ohgrah**fee**ah]
graphic arts	*grafismo*	[grah**fee**smoh]
history	*historia*	[ees**toh**reeah]
journalism	*periodismo*	[pehreeoh**dee**zmoh]
languages	*lenguas*	[**lehn**gwahs]
law	*derecho*	[deh**reh**choh]
literature	*literatura*	[leetehrah**too**rah]
medicine	*medicina*	[mehdee**see**nah]
nursing	*enfermería*	[ehnfehrmeh**ree**ah]
nutrition	*dietética*	[dyehteh**tee**kah]
political science	*ciencias políticas*	[**syehn**syahs poh**lee**teekahs]
psychology	*psicología*	[seekohloh-**hee**ah]
tourism	*turismo*	[too**ree**smoh]

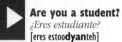

Are you a student?
¿Eres estudiante?
[eres estoo**dyan**teh]

What do you study?
¿Qué estudias?
[keh es**too**dyahs]

FAMILY – *FAMILIA*

brother	*hermano*	[ehr**mah**noh]
brother-in-law	*cuñado*	[koo**nyah**doh]
cousin	*primo/a*	[**pree**moh/ah]
daughter	*hija*	[**ee**hah]
father	*padre*	[**pah**dreh]
grandfather	*abuelo*	[ah**bweh**loh]
grandmother	*abuela*	[ah**bweh**lah]
mother	*madre*	[**mah**dreh]
my brothers and sisters	*mis hermanos*	[meehs ehr**mah**nohs]
nephew	*sobrino*	[soh**bree**noh]
niece	*sobrina*	[soh**bree**nah]
sister	*hermana*	[ehr**mah**nah]
sister-in-law	*cuñada*	[koo**nyah**dah]
son	*hijo*	[**ee**hoh]

SENSATIONS AND EMOTIONS –
SENSACIONES Y EMOCIONES

I am hungry.	*Tengo hambre.*	[**tehn**goh **ahm**breh]
We are hungry.	*Tenemos hambre.*	[teh**neh**mohs **ahm**breh]
He is hungry.	*Él tiene hambre.*	[ehl tye**neh ahm**breh]
She is hungry.	*Ella tiene hambre.*	[**eh**yah **tyeh**neh **ahm**breh]
I am thirsty.	*Tengo sed.*	[**tehn**goh seh]
I am tired.	*Estoy cansado/a.*	[eh**stoy** kahn**sah**doh/ah]
I am cold.	*Tengo frío.*	[**tehn**goh **free**oh]
I am hot.	*Tengo calor.*	[**tehn**goh kah**lor**]
I am sick.	*Estoy enfermo/a.*	[eh**stoy** ehn**fehr**moh/ah]
I am happy.	*Estoy contento/a.* *Soy feliz.*	[eh**stoy** kohn**tehn**toh/ah | soy feh**lees**]
I am satisfied.	*Estoy satisfecho/a.*	[eh**stoy** sahtees**feh**choh/ah]
I am sorry.	*Lo siento.*	[loh **syehn**toh]
I am disappointed.	*Estoy defraudado/a.*	[eh**stoy** dehfrah-oo**dah**doh/ah]
I am bored.	*Me aburro.*	[meh ah**boor**roh]
I have had enough.	*Es suficiente.*	[ehs soofee**syehn**teh]
I cannot wait to...	*Estoy impaciente de...*	[eh**stoy** eempah**syehn**teh deh]

Human Relations

I am getting impatient.	*Me impaciento.*	[meh eempah**syehn**toh]
I am curious about...	*Tengo curiosidad de...*	[**tehn**goh koo-reeohsee**dah** deh]
I am lost.	*Estoy perdido/a.*	[estoy pehr**dee**doh/ah]

Index

162

SPANISH WORDS

NOTES

NOTES

NOTES